THE GA[ ]
TWO WORLDS

Dear Frank,

Thank You!

Wishing you all
the best in
your retirement.

K. M.

9/20/16

What People are Saying About

THE GAP *between* TWO WORLDS

The Gap Between Two Worlds is a compelling account of how the challenges we all face in the inevitable life transitions we experience can become some of our greatest assets. Kevin McNulty offers an engaging account of not only common responses to transition, but very practical strategies for how we can grow through these experiences. For a fast changing world in which transitions are increasing in scope and number, this book offers timely help. Instead of being caught without language or understanding in the normal process of change, readers will find the way through to the strengths these changes can also offer them. I recommend it highly!

RUTH E. VAN REKEN
CO-AUTHOR, *THIRD CULTURE KIDS: GROWING UP AMONG WORLDS*
CO-FOUNDER, FAMILIES IN GLOBAL TRANSITION, INC.

"Kevin McNulty is a 20-year military veteran—turned private sector speaker and author—who knows all too well about navigating a major life change and turning it into a meaningful personal growth experience. I knew Kevin when he was a member of the Air Force, where he demonstrated his unique ability to bring out the best in everyone around him. Through his new book "The Gap Between Two Worlds", he continues to bring out the best in everyone who reads it and takes his message to heart. It's a must read not only for our troops who are immersed in constant change, but also for anyone navigating through a major life transition."

GENERAL TONY ROBERTSON
U.S. AIR FORCE (RETIRED)

Dealing with life's transitions can either renew our life's purpose or cause us to lose our way. This book speaks deep truth about our need to spend time in the gap between the old world and new world...time that enables us to slow down, to understand who we are, to face our fears, to grow, to dream. Filled with questions that challenged my thinking, this book encouraged me to persevere and to pursue my deepest dreams. Kevin McNulty has written a book destined to be a must read for everyone who finds themselves in the Gap.

NANCY REECE
INTEGRITY FANATIC, THE HUMAN CAPITAL GROUP, INC.

Rarely does a book come along that takes such a puzzling topic as personal change & transition and make sense of it the way that Kevin McNulty has so eloquently done in his book *The Gap Between Two Worlds.* Using vivid visuals, empathy and humor, Kevin journey's into that sometimes foggy place—between the old familiar world and the new world that lies ahead—and shows you how much opportunity and meaning is found in transition. Rich with strikingly keen observations and thought-provoking questions about how we choose to handle life transitions, this book is a lantern and a map in your hands to advance you out of the fog and into a new world of self-discovery and enlightenment.

LORRAINE BELLO
PRESIDENT, CO-OWNER
RICKLIN-ECHIKSON ASSOCIATES

We know change is an inevitable part of life, but still it takes us by surprise and sometimes sends us spinning out of control. After experiencing the loss of my daughter, best friend and father within a short period of time, I felt just that, out of control and confused about where to turn next. I am so thankful for the chance to read an advanced copy of Kevin's book *The Gap Between Two Worlds.* It helped me to understand that I could either focus on just "surviving" the transition or I could experience in "The Gap" an opportunity to become an even stronger person. With Kevin's help, I found a sense of direction and purpose, and I am advancing toward a future filled with love and significance.

JOHN BENTLEY
PRESIDENT, POWER 2 TRANSFORM

In these trying times we can all use a healthy dose of wisdom, insight and common sense. Kevin McNulty's book *The Gap Between Two Worlds* is a great place to start. This book will empower you to view change not as something to be feared, but as an opportunity to identify and tackle some of life's challenging issues.

ROBIN CROW
CEO OF DARK HORSE INSTITUTE

If you are anticipating or experiencing a difficult life transition and are not sure where to turn for help, start with this book. Transition and personal development coach Kevin McNulty helped me through a very challenging time in my life when I moved from Italy to Miami, Florida, and he shares his extraordinary knowledge, experience and strategy for transitioning successfully through life in this profound, humorous and practical book, *The Gap Between Two Worlds*.

ANGELO D'AMBRA
OWNER, A STAR IN THE COOKIE JAR

The Gap Between Two Worlds shows us how to learn and grow from life's many adversities. Such knowledge is timeless."

DR. GREGG STEINBERG
AUTHOR OF *FULL THROTTLE*
(WASHINGTON POST BEST SELLER)

THE GAP *between* TWO WORLDS

Turning Difficult Life Transitions
Into Personal Growth Experiences

Kevin Richard McNulty

Humadyn Life Skills Institute
Murfreesboro, Tennessee

The Gap Between Two Worlds: Turning Difficult Life Transitions into Personal Growth Experiences

Published by Humadyn Life Skills Institute
Murfreesboro, TN

Disclaimer

This book is designed to provide information and motivation to the readers. It is sold with the understanding that the author or publisher is not engaged to render any type of psychological, legal, or any other kind of professional advice. If psychological, medical, or other expert assistance is needed, the services of a competent professional should be sought.

Every effort has been made to make this book as complete and accurate as possible. However, there might be mistakes, both typographical and in content. Therefore, this text should be used only as a general guide, and not as the ultimate source when it comes to change and transition or other areas with respect to personal development.

No warranties or guarantees are expressed or implied by the author or publisher to include any of the content in this book. Neither the publisher nor the author shall be liable for any physical, psychological, emotional, financial, or commercial damages, including, but not limited to, special, incidental, consequential, or other damages.

If you do not wish to be bound by the above, you may return this book to the publisher for a full refund.

ISBN 978-0-9856962-2-1 - perfectbound
ISBN 978-0-9856962-3-8 - hardcover
ISBN 978-0-9856962-4-5 - ePub
Library of Congress Control Number: 2012941250

Dedication

To my wife and best friend, Jane E. McNulty,
Who inspired me to write this book and who inspires me every day.

To my children, Kevin II, Christina, and Alexandra,
Who bring so much joy and meaning to my life. I simply adore you.

To my father, Charles M. McNulty,
Who, through his military service, made many transitions—and
gave immeasurably to our country.

To Maynard and Nancy Johnson and family,
Who have endured an incredible transition with such grace.

In Loving Memory

My mother,
Nereida Antonia Reyes (Martin) McNulty

and

My nephew,
Alexander McNulty

Epigraph

"I have learned to trust the processes that take time, to value change that is not sudden or ill-considered but grows out of the ground of experience. Such change is properly defined as conversion, a word that at its root connotes not a change of essence but of perspective"

—Kathleen Norris, Dakota: A Spiritual Geography

Acknowledgments

Writing this book was like traveling a long and winding road with many detours and diversions. Although I sometimes complained [to myself] about this very tasking process, I've come to realize that things were always unfolding as they should. Through the course of researching and writing this book, I've had the privilege of crossing paths with hundreds of people who knowingly or not enriched my life. To you all, I am so grateful.

First, I give thanks to God for giving me the wherewithal to write this book, and that it be an instrument of His purpose.

Further, I want to thank the following people:

My wife Jane (Johnson) McNulty, partner, and soul mate who helped me in so many ways that I don't know where to begin—and if I did, it would take writing another book to spell it all out.

My longtime best friends, George Spotts, Doug Allen, and John Bentley, whose amazing friendships and counsel have been immeasurable.

The many "transition guides" who, knowingly or not, helped me during my transition from my military career: my brothers and sister (Chuck, Chester, Sharon, and Edgar) and their families; my in-law family (The Johnsons)—and, particularly, to my mother-in-law (Nancy) who guided my family and me in so many ways.

My good friends and colleagues, Louise Olszewski, Steve Jones, and Cathy Harris who helped me when throwing in the towel on my business was imminent.

My editor and writing coach, C. Leslie Charles, who pushed me to be a better writer and who brought such a wonderful perspective and eloquent edits to my story and ideas.

Jason Ehleben (cover art), Susan Andres (copy editor), and Kim Leonard (cover/interior design); Dean Heasley, Jay Hottel, Nancy Johnson, Betty Childress, and Sue Redmond (manuscript reviewers); Melissa Hines, Mark Johnson, and Rebecca Holly Ary for helping me with some important details in the final stretch.

To all (including anyone I've forgotten) I am so grateful. Thank you!

Table of Contents:

Foreword

There is one thing that remains constant in life, and that is change. Change can be scary, but change brings opportunity. The chance to evolve and morph into a more successful being by utilizing what could hold you back in a fashion that propels you forward is what this book is prepared to teach you.

You are holding a golden key that will help to unlock a natural fear in your psyche that can keep us all from achieving our dreams. Use this book to understand that you can handle change and transition in your life. Eventually, you learn to change from within because of your circumstances. You grow, mature, and prosper because of your life experiences that make you stronger.

As this book outlines, there are transitions in life that appear to be threatening. They may be things that happened because of our actions. Or they could be the result of something beyond our control.

Either way, we cannot control and must not resist change. We must face it head on by embracing it and using it in some way for our advantage.

I came to this country at the age of 17 speaking little English and with only $50. My goal of pursuing a college career and achieving the American dream was at the top of my priority list. But, I faced numerous obstacles, both financial and personal, that could have prevented me from achieving my goal. I persevered through decisions that for many people would have been too difficult or uncomfortable to make.

We must realize that taking calculated risks in life is what all successful people must do. One must look at each decision and say, can I live with the worst thing that will happen? Can I live with the best thing that will happen? In most situations, what happens is something squarely in the middle of those two.

Sometimes, however, things may not go your way. But, the knowledge that decisions may not turn out well all the time should never hold you back from making calculated risks that can advance you forward in your professional career or your personal life.

Success does not come to you, you must go to it. The path is well-traveled, but we must take the appropriate steps that will take us where we need—and want—to be.

In my career as a professional speaker and consultant and now as president of High Point University, I have learned that when you arm yourself with the information you need to make informed and wise decisions, the pathway to growth and success becomes clear.

At High Point University, we model values and focus on a holistic educational experience so that students graduate with a well-rounded thought process and ambitious plan for life. Values-based learning is imperative to one's career and personal development.

We arm our students with the thought process that they are prepared to make important, and sometimes risky, decisions in their life in the effort to grow and prosper. And, we also arm them with the tools they need to understand how to convert challenges in their lives to opportunity. Often, it is what we push against that can lift us up.

Like the wind, when a plane flies into the wind at full throttle, it is lifted up to greater heights.

This book is an invaluable tool that will help propel you towards your goals and lift you to greater heights in all that you do.

Dr. Nido Qubein
President, High Point University
Chairman, Great Harvest Bread Co.
www.NidoQubein.com

Introduction

Why I Wrote This Book

A few years ago while flying to Florida, I sat next to an old, very wise rabbi talking about life. At one point, he said, "Kevin, we make plans, and God just laughs."

This book begins with the premise that there are no secrets or magic formulas to transitioning successfully in life. Each transition is different with unique nuances and circumstances. However, I have learned through my experiences and research that many challenges and principles for success are the same, no matter what the transition.

This book was spawned from my many, and often extraordinary, experiences in dealing with change and transition. However, I began to research this topic after one of my most challenging transitions from a 20-year, highly structured, military lifestyle to a very different one—that of a private citizen. If you also count my nearly 20 years as a military brat moving around the world every 2 years and similarly living in a structured military household, then you can better grasp that becoming a private citizen at age 40 was truly a new world, a foreign land for me. Concisely, I felt as though I had moved to another planet.

We can make anything sound simple, but in this case, I've concluded that major life transitions can be very complicated. However, I hope in this book to make sense of it all and to communicate the complexities of change and transition into a simple, straightforward, and practical way.

It's a State of Mind

I will discuss this in detail later, but for now, your state of mind and the conditions preceding your transition play significantly into how your transition unfolds. For me, not only 40 years of structure preceded my transition, but also a career in which I earnestly thrived. I was on top of my game and progressing in a positive direction. I enjoyed my work and life. I valued my work and felt valued. However, I had come to a place in my heart and mind where I knew my life needed to move in a different direction. As a person also maturing spiritually, I felt strongly that God was telling me, "Move on, Kevin! There is other work for you."

I loved my military life—the diversity of people, camaraderie, travel, security, and stability that came with it. More, it was all I'd ever known. But I can also say that not a day went by that I didn't have the thought that although I was doing important and rewarding work in the Air Force, I had another purpose and dream to fulfill, and eventually, I would have to move away from the military. Right around the 20-year mark, although I was deathly afraid of making the transition, I knew it was time. In retrospect, I can see that what I loved about my "old world" (my military life) would in part become what caused such a challenge in my transition.

The Creep Factor

Practically, I knew that my transition to civilian life was inevitable in a few years, so I decided to transition sooner rather than later. Further, I knew from speaking to colleagues who had already "crossed-over" into civilian life that my transition would be difficult and for a host of reasons. So, in preparing for my transition, I committed substantial time and effort toward preparation. When I finally transitioned, I felt very confident and prepared for a significant career and life transition.

For the first several weeks following my transition—this midlife career change—from the Air Force, I experienced a nervous honeymoon phase. I more or less felt as if I was on vacation. I took the long drive from California to Tennessee where my family had already moved. After arriving, I mostly spent time with my wife Jane and two young daughters, Christina Ariel, nearly 5, and Alexandra Jane, 1½. During that period, I shifted between a little edgy and bored, but for the most part, I celebrated and appreciated my newfound freedom as a private citizen.

However, in the months to come, my state of mind began to change. It happened slowly, but I began to shift into a general state of uncertainty—about everything. It was subtle at first. Later, I became more confused and concerned, then frustrated, and eventually depressed.

As I moved forward, the reality and characteristics of my new life began to reveal themselves. Perhaps it's better to say that the reality of my loss became evident, but it "crept up" on me. The familiar support systems, the language and jargon, conversations, structure, and friends were just not there. The basic losses of a familiar personal and professional interaction and stimulation were gone, and they left a void.

Get Me Out of Here!

The more I faced this new world, the more vulnerable I felt. I had dreams—really nightmares—of standing on a stage in front of a large audience naked and saying to myself, "Kevin, why are you just standing here? Get off the stage! Just turn left or right, and walk off the stage!" But for some reason, I couldn't move. In retrospect, I knew this recurring dream was analogous to my real life. I felt vulnerable, indecisive—but also stripped naked and paralyzed.

In my real life, I began to question where my life was going. As in the dream, I was petrified. In a few months, I had gone from my old world, where I felt comfortable, confident, sure-footed, and successful, to a new world, where I seemed to lack any means to move forward with confidence. I was stuck in the gap between two worlds.

For weeks and months, I struggled, as though I was pushing a boulder uphill. I struggled with life on a level I had never experienced. I struggled with my identity, my direction, and heavy emotional turmoil. I'd experienced emotional pain before, but this time, it was different. At the time, I didn't know why or from where the pain was coming. It was as if a dark cloud had moved over me—but it wouldn't pass. My psyche had become my worst enemy.

At many points in my transition, I reached a tipping point. I thought, "Life would be much easier, Kevin, if you would only abandon your dream of becoming a speaker and author and go out and get a real job." I was reaching the point that I just wanted the pain to go away. It seemed that a job—that is, preoccupation—was the cure.

I Cared Too Much

To make matters worse, the chronic stress led to physical illness. I found myself in a health situation that rendered me nearly immobile. What a vicious circle I stepped into—the emotional pain exacerbated my physical pain, and the physical pain exacerbated my emotional pain.

Despite my family near by, I felt lonely and confused. I didn't understand it, nor could I explain it. I felt fear, but I was unsure what I feared—failure, success, the unknown? I later learned that much of this was happening, not because I was emotionally weak, but in part because I cared too much about winning—that is, it mattered so much that I feared failing.

Can you care so much that you reach saturation, and caring becomes futile?

Clear as Mud

Soon, I went from being clear, motivated, and enthusiastic about my future to suddenly looking around and asking myself questions that seemed to have no answers. Things were clear as mud. A good metaphor: It was as though I had planned and painted a clear discernible vision of what my life would look like, and then one day, I looked at the painting, and saw only an abstract illustration that made no sense. I didn't recognize the painting or the painter.

During this time, I indeed became self-aware. I pondered for many days and weeks, asking questions and trying to get a grip. How did this all come to be? Why did I find myself in such difficulty? What was causing this difficulty and pain? Who was I? Where was I going? What was or is my vision, my mission, and my values? There were more questions than answers.

Many times, I had to fight a panicked state of mind. The anxieties tempted me repeatedly to give up and get a regular job to preoccupy my mind and life, but I resisted abandoning even my now not-so-clear vision.

A Breakthrough

After many days of deep, hard introspection and contemplation, I became more conscious and confident that my mind was playing games with me. This understanding was a powerful and pivotal recognition. Then, from encouragement and counsel from Jane (my wife and soul mate), conversations with two of my closest friends George Spotts and Doug Allen, and constant prayer, I slowly began to see my vision again. From there, I began to gain strength and resolve to face and remain steadfast through these difficult times.

If you are in such a difficult transition, this is a key premise to traversing the Gap between your two worlds. As I did, you must learn to lean on faith, family, and friends and to trust them during the temporary blindness. I learned that I had a distorted perception of my life and that I needed to trust. I needed to trust in God who could see the greater good that would come from my struggles. And I had to trust my wife—that she was seeing things clearer than I was about my life and direction. She was an excellent guide.

Getting Back My Mojo

As I began to get back on track, I came to understand the many problems with which I needed to take care. Some were natural consequences of any change and transition, such as the challenges you face when wandering into unknown territory. Other problems were not so much inherent with change or transition but more strictly personal development problems with which I needed to deal, such as immaturity, self-esteem, or identity issues. For instance, for 20 years, I saw myself as a valued member of an organization and culture; but when I moved away from that world, in effect, I was nothing. I had no rank, no status, no identity; no one needed my skills and expertise. I just became a self-absorbed victim. I had lost my "mojo."

Most important, once I got hold of my mind, I could see these problems, separate them, deal with them, and learn from them, which is when the personal growth took off. I almost couldn't keep up with the fast and many life lessons that came my way. The truth is, the lessons—and the lessons from the lessons—continue.

One of my most recent great lessons—and speaking of "mojo"—came from my friend and professional mentor, Dr. Marshall Goldsmith. In his book, MOJO: How to Get It, How to Keep It, and How to Get It Back if You Lose It, Marshall defines and offers different ways of thinking about one's mojo. However, what particularly resonated with me was his belief that "the word has evolved to describe a sense of positive spirit and direction, especially in the shifting tides of the sports, business, and politics." We can add "transitions" to this list. We can sometimes lose our way, our positive spirit, and direction during a major transition. The keyword to hang on to here, however, is shift—because although we can inadvertently shift and lose our mojo, we can also shift and get back our mojo.

Pass It On

An executive that I coach said something that astonished me. About halfway through this yearlong leadership-coaching program, Steve came to me and said, "Kevin, this program has been life-changing for me. I've learned things that have helped me immeasurably. My only problem is that I feel a bit selfish that I'm doing this for my self-improvement." He then asked, "What can I do to pass these concepts and practices on to my employees?" His intent through that question epitomizes what should happen when we learn, grow, and become a better person—you become and act like a better person.

Although change and transition are the topics of this book, I hope you see that it really has to do with self-discovery and personal growth, which is why the subtitle states Turning Difficult Life Transitions into Personal Growth Experiences. I don't recommend that you enter a major traumatic change so you can "find yourself." However, if you are in a major transition or expecting one, know that there is a great silver lining. The lessons that you can and that you will find in the Gap are like none other. Nido Qubein, one of today's great communicators and success thought-leaders, says, "Change brings opportunity." I can assure you that the Gap brings a worthy and sometimes life-changing opportunity to discover who you are.

Finally, once you gain this hard-won wisdom from traversing the Gap, pass it on. This book is my attempt to do just that.

Chapter 1

The Gap Between Two Worlds

Every moment of one's existence one is growing into more or retreating into less.

— **Norman Mailer**

Maybe you've heard someone describe a nightmarish tale about surviving cancer or getting divorced, yet after recounting their struggles, the person utters in an awed tone, "I wouldn't be who I am today without having gone through it." Perhaps this conclusion stunned you. At one time, I just couldn't wrap my mind around such a paradoxical statement.

But I can now. I now often find myself echoing those sentiments when describing my journey. After facing a series of upheavals and the daunting disruption that hard times can bring, I ended up with a life-changing transformation I wouldn't trade for anything. Though painful at the time, my struggles helped me realize that times of difficulty, transition, or crisis are the route to self-discovery and personal development. In other words, the very distress that holds us in its grip and forces us to take stock is our pathway toward insight, understanding, and finally, personal reinvention.

One of our problems with change (or crisis) is that many of us don't realize a truth that deep inside every adversity is an opportunity if we are willing to take the leap. Most of the time when things get uncomfortable, we scurry away from the turmoil as fast as we can instead of gearing up and plowing through it. Perhaps human nature makes us want to avoid the unknown, unpredictable, or unwanted, but there's a better way.

Granted, we human beings have an instinct to gravitate toward what feels good (even if it's only temporary) and avoid pain whenever possible—you know the drill. And I'll be the first to admit that struggling with a major life transition is no walk in the park. Coming face to face with great change can be physically and emotionally grueling, whether we choose it, or it chooses us. It's uncomfortable. It hurts. It's a lot of work. It takes time. And it's as natural and essential to being alive as is breathing.

My transition unearthed a hotbed of emotions I didn't know what to do with and an emotional minefield I wasn't sure I could safely navigate. I couldn't shake this pervading sense of loss; and the worst part was the feeling that I had lost a grip on me. It was as if who I was had slipped away somehow, but as time passed, I truly found myself in that gaping black hole. And (I hope you're ready for this) I wouldn't have missed it for the world!

Just Do It!

When facing a personal hardship and psychological challenges, sometimes, all we want to do is gut it out and get through it—forget the learning—just close your eyes, hit fast forward, and hold on. But there's a price to pay for taking life's express lane, and the toll is just not worth it. The word transition is a synonym for progress, evolution, metamorphosis, changeover, and transformation. If we rush through a change, challenge, or life passage with our heads down and our mental blinders fixed in place, we unknowingly short-circuit the natural process of taking our lives (and our potential) to the next level. When we focus on the past or rush into the future unprepared because we fear or loathe the present, we sacrifice the valuable and lasting lessons there for the taking.

In other words, trying to deny, avoid, or rush the process means we can't possibly absorb the learning and emotional expansion occurring as we slowly (and yes, sometimes painfully) shift from where we are to where we want (or need) to be. Please know that I completely understand the appeal of the "accelerated" approach—it's exactly what I tried to do in the beginning of my transition. And it didn't work. I found a better way, one that does work, which is why I wrote this book.

Your World Series

Here's what I had to learn—life is a series of transitions. Some are small (buying a new car, rearranging a room as one of our children moves out or back in), and some are significant (graduating from school and going out on your own, moving to a new area, marrying or divorcing, recovering from an accident or illness). Some transitions are easier than others are. Some are smooth, and some are rough; but here's the reality—it might take a while for them to surface, but the *major* life transitions, the big ones, are inevitable.

3

It's not enough to cope or halfheartedly deal with change because the point isn't to survive the experience. The point is learning how to brace yourself so you can accept the circumstances, deal with the discomfort you feel, internalize the insights as they come to you, and eventually thrive because of what you've gone through. Each time you face a hardship, conflict, or turning point in your life, the opportunity exists for you to transform who you are. In other words, as you emerge from your life shift or transition, whether it's one you chose or one imposed on you, you'll discover that you have a new skill set and perspective you didn't have before. It's a powerful and empowering experience.

You are probably familiar with the life cycle of the lobster and its shedding its old shell and developing a new one so it can continue to grow and evolve. A lobster's shell is hard and inelastic, restricting any growth. If the creature couldn't get rid of its shell, it would die (this might cause you to think of people you know whose attitudes are so rigid they haven't made any kind of personal changes in decades). The lobster goes through several molts (or shell changes) yearly, which is its built-in survival mechanism. Perhaps we could consider flexibility and the willingness to adjust to new circumstances as essential survival skills in the ever-changing world we now find ourselves.

As you can imagine, the lobster is vulnerable and in flux during the transition period of its molt and maybe you can probably think of times in your life you felt that way. The good news is that change and reconstruction are integral to our existence. Never doubt that we are mentally and physically up to the task; it's in our genetic code. And it might help to add that a synonym for the word *change* is *advance*. Believe me when I say I was no change rock star when I faced the biggest transition in my life, which will be confirmed as you read along. But if I could successfully advance through my wormhole and

4

come out a better person on the other side, so can you. The key is in anticipating and understanding what's inside a process I call *the Gap*.

Meet the Gap

What I call "the Gap between two worlds" constitutes everything we experience when we face the inevitable changes, challenges, and transitions that occur during our lifetime. The Gap involves three major parts that apply to nearly any transition, large or small:

1. **The Old World:** This is our old life, the way things used to be: the known, the familiar, and the predictable.
2. **The New World:** This is the way things will be awhile: the unknown, the uncharted, the unpredictable, and the unrevealed new life into which we will eventually ease.
3. **The Gap:** We must navigate this period of transition between our two worlds, the one we're leaving and the one we will enter. The Gap is a fuzzy period of space and time existing between the old world and the new one; that is, you hover between the world as you once knew it and the new unmapped, uncharted world before you.

Although at first glance, the Gap might seem nothing more than an in-between stage of transition, it's far more than that. It's your vision quest, a pivotal moment in your journey. It's a test of your endurance, your ability to handle ambiguity, and an opportunity to explore your threshold of resilience. In the beginning, the Gap may be a place riddled with turmoil, uncertainty, unpredictability, isolation, fear, and self-doubt. When the journey is complete, the Gap becomes profuse in enlightenment, self-empowerment, insight, connection, and inner peace. Working your way through the Gap might not be the kind of experience you would wish for, but it's filled with the kind of revelation that brings you a deeper sense of confidence, expanded self-knowledge, and newly gained wisdom that will serve you for the rest of your life.

Every transition, despite its depth or breadth, involves a trip through the Gap. The period spent in shifting from the old world to the new might be brief or protracted, depending on the circumstances and the person. A career change, geographic relocation, the beginning or end of a significant relationship, the onset of a major illness, loss of a loved one, retirement, and even the transition from high school to college, or college to the workplace, are just some transitions we might encounter on our life's journey. Some transitions are more significant than others are, and a few are traumatic until we regain our sense of equilibrium.

> *Difficult times, transitions, or crisis can pave a path to self-discovery and personal development.*

At first, it might be tempting to say that this all is just common sense, but there's more to navigating transitions than meets the eye. What might be smooth sailing for one person might be turbulent or traumatic for another. Transitions are often tricky, and sometimes, we don't realize their impact until we're well on the other side and have the luxury of looking back. Only then, we realize some of the obvious, that we had more choices than we thought or more inner strength than we knew, and if we had realized what was on the other side, we wouldn't have waited so long to act. In this book, I outline the Gap process, including signals or symptoms to watch for so you can make your transitions less difficult for you and those you love.

Please remember that the lines are often blurry in exactly where a transition begins and ends. Just to keep things simple, let's agree that a transition starts once you become aware that change has occurred or is about to occur. Trust yourself and trust the process of advancement; you'll feel the shift.

The Two Worlds

A variety of elements and circumstances will affect the size and gravity of your Gap. Transitions are difficult. We must trade old ways of behaving for new ones, even if the change is something we want. Then, there are the complications of changes forced on us—the times we're forced to grapple with circumstances we didn't want, ask for, expect, or imagine would ever happen to us. Those are the most challenging circumstances of all. But whether we made the choice or it was made for us, we will sometimes find ourselves suspended in the Gap between those two worlds—the old, familiar one and the new, unknown one yet uncharted. That's what this book is about.

The two worlds I describe are not just an intellectual idea. Each world, the old and the new alike, constitute particular people, places, experiences, circumstances, relationships, emotions, beliefs, meanings, and personal perceptions that factor into what you would describe as *your life,* before and after a change.

Below are a few of the most common transitions we human beings typically experience at some point in our lives. As you review these transitions, consider the ones with which you've had firsthand experience and both the difficulties and discoveries you gained along the way.

OLD WORLD	⇒	NEW WORLD
Single	⇒	Married
Married	⇒	Single
High School	⇒	College
College	⇒	Work
Old Job	⇒	New Job
Hometown	⇒	New City
Contentment	⇒	Loss or Death
Active Parenting	⇒	Empty Nester
Vital and Healthy	⇒	Diminishing Capacity

As you have probably deduced, not just the worlds affect the depth or breadth of the Gap, but also what is in those worlds. The quality of experiences in the old world can carry much emotional weight if that world is suddenly no longer there for you. You could be filled with a combination of relief and uncertainty if you've freed yourself from an untenable situation, or you might be sad and rejected if you're the one left. The mental and physical prospects from your old world and the ones that loom in the new world play a major role in the level of challenge you will face during your transition.

Just as the lobster must struggle to free itself of its old, constricting shell, you will face your struggles in the Gap. Expect it, be ready for it, roll up your sleeves, and work your way through it. And as you settle into the domain of your new world and look back at where you once were (and maybe initially wanted to remain), you will find yourself renewed, reaffirmed, and relieved that you're no longer there.

Gaps Vary in Size and Scope

Here are two examples that illustrate the potential fallout of a major life transition as you progress through the Gap.

Situation 1:

You are in a job you enjoy. You've been with the company for 20 years, having worked your way up through the ranks. During your tenure, you have cultivated many close relationships with coworkers, and you feel as if you're the right person in the right job at the right time. In your kind of work, people tend to stay where they are; openings are rare and hard to find. Then, it happens. Boom—you are suddenly laid off with no time to prepare.

Situation 2:

You are employed, though the circumstances differ from what is described above. You don't much like the work or your coworkers, for that matter. You've been with the company for only a year, and if the worst should happen, there are enough other jobs in your field, and you have some connections. Boom—you are suddenly laid off with no time to prepare.

The transition in the first situation would obviously be more challenging than the second would. The shock and confusion, the potential resentment, the time and effort required looking for a new job, and the emotional investment in both your work and people you valued would weigh heavily on your mind. The shake-up of sudden loss and displacement could result in anger, outrage, or even embarrassment that stops you in your tracks. You might feel stymied and lack the desire to update your resume or rally your resources so you can move on. You might lose faith in yourself or the system that treated you so shabbily. You might question why you were released when others with less seniority or specialized skills could stay.

Avoiding or rushing the process means not absorbing the learning and emotional expansion occurring as we shift from where we are to where we want or need to be.

Welcome to one of the Gap's ironies. When you most need inner calm and confidence, you might instead feel daunted and filled with self-doubt as you face the immense chasm filled with unknowns and unresolved problems. Trying to feel your way through the Gap that lies between the world as you knew it and the new unfamiliar, unpredictable world waiting just beyond your grasp is not easy.

The transition in the second situation involves far less emotional or physical stress. Although it might still present some challenges, the personal impact of this transition pales in comparison to the first.

You weren't that crazy about the work or the people around you, and chances are you had thought about making a change. It's likely that you would feel more confident and be more comfortable entering the new world, though you don't know what it will hold for you. Yes, this incident might be inconvenient and a bit worrisome because of its abruptness, but your transition would be much less traumatic than the first would. In this case, other than the job itself, you didn't have much to lose.

When you transition from one world to another, you enter uncharted territory; you have no map to follow. You create your path systematically, and periodically, you must stop, assess where you are, and maybe readjust your direction. That's much of what makes the Gap so challenging. You've temporarily lost your hold on that tenuous thing we call reality, and now, your job is to create one. It's not easy, but you're up to task. I guarantee you.

The greater your investment in the old world, the more challenging your transition into the new world will be.

Two Worlds, a Gap, and No Map

Maybe in reading this chapter, you've recalled some transition in your life and the Gap that accompanied the changes you experienced. Or maybe now, you're getting ready to face a significant shift in your work, lifestyle, or a relationship. If so, I encourage you to consider your circumstances to the best of your ability and review the known conditions that will compose your Gap.

The questions at the end of this chapter can help you think through your situation so you can better understand the possible feelings of loss, isolation, or uncertainty you might experience. Investigate the elements or forces you expect will intensify the discomfort or challenge of the Gap you'll be entering. I heartily recommend that you write your answers to the questions. Not only will you gain some insight about yourself and your situation, but you'll also have notes you can review in the future for identifying what worked (or what didn't) and measuring your progress.

A Vote of Confidence

We human beings are very adaptable, yet most of us resist almost instinctively, even when the change is our choice. If you've ever decided to lose weight, get in shape, or quit smoking, how successful were you right out of the gate? If you're like the rest of us, you had trouble breaking those old habits; it was difficult giving up your old way of being. Yet, if you ended up achieving your goal, things changed. Your world changed because you changed. You left your old-world ways behind and embraced new-world behaviors.

In successfully making it through the Gap, you got thinner, stronger, or healthier, and I'll bet you gained new self-knowledge along the way. Maybe you got in touch with your stalwart sense of determination and willingness to gut it through the uncomfortable, unsure period where you weren't sure you'd make it. Chances are your self-confidence increased as you measured your progress, and maybe you even discovered new strategies for setting and achieving your goals. In short, by transitioning into your new world (no matter what it took), you transformed something in yourself and became a more balanced, well-rounded person.

Life is a series of transitions.

If you are in the middle of, or expecting, a significant transition, take some time to consider as many elements about both your old world and the new one that waits. Plan how you will handle the pressure of the Gap, that period of ambiguity and instability that will invariably mess with your lofty goals. This is not merely an intellectual exercise.

Just as you would pack a first-aid kit if you were going on a back-packing trip, you want to be as prepared as possible for whatever happens, from the best and the worst. The Gap is a real place and time; it's not a theory. And the more of yourself and your resources you can take with you into the Gap, the better.

Summary of "The Gap Between Two Worlds":

- Times of difficulty, transition, or crisis are the routes to self-discovery and personal development.
- Trying to deny, avoid, or rush the process means we can't possibly absorb the learning and emotional expansion occurring as we shift from where we are to where we want or need to be.
- Life is a series of transitions.
- Each time you face a hardship, conflict, or turning point in your life, the opportunity exists for you to transform who you are.
- The Gap involves three major parts: the old world, the new world, and the Gap itself.
- Every transition involves a trip through the Gap.
- Each world, the old and the new alike, constitutes particular people, places, experiences, circumstances, relationships, emotions, beliefs, meanings, and personal perceptions that factor into what you would describe as *your life,* before and after a change.
- Gaps vary in size and scope.
- Not just the worlds affect the depth or breadth of the Gap, but also what is in those worlds.
- If you are in the middle of, or expecting, a significant transition, take some time to consider as many elements about both your old world and the new one that waits and to plan for the Gap.

Personal Reflections:

1. Take a moment to reflect on one of your more chaotic or painful experiences with change.

   - How could you have prepared better for the challenge?
   - What do you wish you had known before the process began?
   - With what you know now, would you have handled it differently?

2. Is there a change in your future? Like the lobster that grows a thin protective shell before it casts off the old one, consider what you might need during that vulnerability to help fortify or protect you.

   - What part of your old world are you ready (and maybe even relieved) to let go of, and why?
   - Will it leave a void, and with what will you fill the void?
   - What are your "survival strategies" for coping with this change, loss, or alteration of your status?
   - How can you best prepare for this transition—what do you need to do before you move forward, and if you need help, who might be able to help you?

Chapter 2

A Glimpse Inside the Gap

Transitioning from the old to the new world involves a personal odyssey, your individualized pilgrimage through the Gap. It's a solo expedition that will expose you to some of life's grittier elements, unearthing many emotional, social, and physical challenges plus some transformative insights you would never otherwise gain. Your situation's complexity will influence the size, intensity, and duration of this turbulent period I call the Gap. The level of your openness and willingness to persevere and embrace or internalize your lessons will determine how much you (and your life) transform.

Not all transitions are life changing, but every new experience comes with its set of emotional, social, or physical aspects. For instance, consider the factors that might exist for a high school graduate transitioning to college.

The student might be

- Excited about the prospect of getting a degree (or not)
- Looking forward to getting away from home (or not)
- Happy to quit being so dependent on parents for about everything (or not)
- Content to be living at home and driving across town for classes (or not)
- Exhilarated at the thought of moving to a foreign country on a one-year scholarship program (or not)

There are emotional, social, and physical issues related to beleaguered scholars whose parents doggedly insist on higher education at an Ivy League school or the community college freshmen delighted at being first in the family to advance beyond high school. In all these situations, you can appreciate how particular factors alter the course of the transition and its inherent challenges. In your situation, you can appreciate the need to understand and address every identifiable factor to the best of your ability so you can maintain stability as your world begins to shape-shift and mutate.

Transition and Loss

In moving away from the old world and into the Gap, you'll inevitably leave things. Loss is a built-in component of a transition. The extent of the loss is proportional to the depth or breadth of the Gap you face, whether it's an exciting prospect or unexpected adversity. The losses connected to transitions often take us off guard. We might think we were prepared for all contingencies (I did), but soon, we discover the void or unintended consequences that come with the territory, and it takes us by surprise.

Imagine a family preparing to move, and consider how a single factor (distance for example) causes the Gap to widen or deepen and present different levels of challenge to each family member. You'll no doubt recognize that however hard we might try to prepare for all contingencies, we cannot predict, control, or fully manage the full effect of some transitional aspects, as we might like.

1. **The family moves from their house to a new home in a different neighborhood but in the same town.**
2. **The family moves from their hometown to a nearby town.**
3. **The family moves from their home state to a bordering state.**
4. **The family moves from California to Mississippi.**
5. **The family moves from Vermont to Italy.**

In each situation, distance alters the nature of the move. The farther the distance, the greater the potential loss intensifying the size of the Gap each family member will face. It's not the distance itself, but related changes that affect the emotional, social, and physical aspects of the move. Considerations such as the extent of preparation or length of the adjustment period and whether the change is chosen or imposed can affect the intensity of emotion. The adults might fare better than the children who have no voice in the move. Each member of the moving family will face the Gap and its repercussions from his or her perspective and circumstances.

The more time a person has spent in the old world, the harder the transition can be. After years of emotional and physical investment, this person will need time for letting go or moving away from how things once were. Anyone diagnosed with a chronic illness, facing the end of a long-term relationship, or going through a contentious divorce must reckon with losses. With death or divorce, not only does a person lose a partner, he or she might also lose the friendship of best-friend couples who are uncomfortable spending time with a single person.

Divorce or death can involve having to let go of anger or resentment, as a person is forced to deal with new routines or daily challenges their partner once handled. Illness requires letting go of the past and adjusting to a "new normal" that might be limiting, time consuming, or expensive. Not all transitions are so dire, but the Gap quickly teaches us the distinctions between the old world and the new. To give you hope, let me remind you that experiencing loss and letting go can release a wealth of enlightening lessons that only come through adversity. We draw on strength we didn't know we had; we discover how resilient the human spirit can be. We find new dimensions of our character that would otherwise never have surfaced; we become wiser, deeper, and more empathetic toward others in similar situations.

The less familiar we are with the new world awaiting us the more turbulent our Gap will be. Adapting to an uncomfortable new reality or a highly unpredictable circumstance requires much time, thought, and energy, and some of us suffer from impatience or annoyance instead of endurance. It's an experience you can't ignore or accelerate. Even a happy change might require adjustment time because everything in the new world is so different from the old. Consider a bride's post-wedding letdown once the intricately planned and highly awaited Big Day is over or the "Now what?" feeling that might set in after a hard-won, long-term goal is met. Even positive transitions can be tricky.

A Comparison of Change and Transition

The most discerning statement I've come across about change and transition came from author William Bridges from his 1991 book, *Managing Transitions: Making the Most of Change.* He said, "It isn't the changes that do you in, it's the transitions." He went on to define change as situational and that transition is the psychological process people go through to come to terms with the new situation.

It is indeed important to distinguish change from transition; being able to recognize the difference between the two will help you better know exactly what you are dealing with and how you are managing it.

Change can best be understood as a turning point or moment in time. Think of it as an event or the event, which makes change easier to identify. Change involves a decision, incident, or an act that sets the transition in motion. The following examples are illustrations of change, as I like to define it.

A Dark Subject

You are in a lighted room, and you turn the lights off. Turning off the lights is the act that causes the change (light to dark). Your action is the catalyst that sets the transition in motion. For a few minutes, everything is dark and indistinguishable, but then your eyes and mind adjust to the new conditions. Even if you used a dimmer to turn the lights down, the change would still occur, only more slowly and smoothly. Once you turn the lights out, the dark room is the new world, whereas the illuminated room represents what existed in the old world.

Loss is a built-in component of a transition.

Happily Ever After

After a long courtship, a widow and widower marry. They decide to move into the widower's house because it has more room and a nicer yard. The change occurs when the widow's possessions are packed and moved into her new home. However, the widow has a difficult time with the transition because she can't stop thinking about her old house and the memories it held, the years she spent raising her children, and more. The widower is also having his adjustment period. After decades of living with his first wife, he struggles to keep old memories while making space for his new wife.

Both of these newlyweds find themselves in their versions of the Gap between two worlds as they try to resolve how things used to be and how they are now (or are becoming). If you face any significant change, do what you can to anticipate, plan for, and manage circumstances before the fact. Once the change has occurred, you are then in transition; you're on your journey, and you will face known and unknown elements that will influence you and yours.

Perhaps before their wedding, the couple could have talked with a counselor or minister about the changes they were about to make in their lives and awkward or uncomfortable feelings the transition period would bring. Too often, we only focus on change as an isolated instance and forget the adjustment period (the transition) that will inevitably follow and take us by surprise.

The Price of Freedom

I once watched an unforgettable documentary about a federal prison inmate released from prison after a 25-year sentence. Talk about an abrupt change that would require an intense transition period! Within moments, it was apparent that this happy occasion would bring many unexpected challenges. In attempting to get into the car for his ride home, the man struggled with the handle design; it was so foreign he had no clue how to open the car door. Although the released inmate was incredibly happy about leaving prison, the documentary catalogued many social changes that had occurred during his incarceration. He would need to make all kinds of adjustments during his transition to the everyday world. The Gap between his old world of prison life and the new world awaiting him loomed deep and wide.

Transition: It's a Part of Life

I think of transition periods as unavoidable journeys connected to a notable event or change requiring an adjustment period. We are familiar with these experiences. You have already gone through all kinds of changes and shifts in your life. Transitions are inescapable. Some are smooth; some are challenging; and some are life changing.

The early stages of transitions involve facing a series of practical, doable tasks often complicated by emotional issues. For example, if you move to another country, you must deal with many hands-on activities and to-do items, from packing and unpacking to getting used to driving on the "wrong" side of the road to learning a new language and adjusting to a foreign culture. Then, there are the move's emotional aspects. I define emotional issues during times of transition as involving feelings such as sadness, anger, or frustration. A body of research concludes that change or transition can trigger psychological issues such as anxiety or clinical depression, but for the sake of simplicity, I will restrict my comments to the emotional issues or conflicts always embedded in a transition.

One Woman's Journey

I once coached a client (and now my friend) though a very challenging personal and career transition. Viviane was born and raised in France. She worked as a consultant for a prestigious firm in Paris. Her husband worked for a large corporation, and he was offered a new position in Los Angeles, California. Together, the couple decided that he would accept the position, and they moved from Paris to LA. This was a huge change in both their lives, especially Viviane's. In a flash, she experienced a change in culture, country, and employment. The practical aspects of these changes were difficult but identifiable and doable. Viviane first had to strengthen her English language skills. Then, she began to adjust consciously to the functions of every-day life she could once take for granted and face without a thought. Her new everyday world involved everything from using differently designed doorknobs or shower handles to all sorts of basic systems, processes and procedures those already accustomed may take for granted. Viviane was inundated with a preponderance of unfamiliar products in the supermarket and intimidated by the ever-present, confusing road signs on the LA freeway. She also had to learn the American way of searching for a new job.

As if the practical aspects of her move weren't enough, the emotional toll of Viviane's transition far overshadowed the down-to-earth adjustments she had to make. She suffered the loss of family and friends and daily rituals or activities that had once brought her comfort, satisfaction, or a sense of belonging. She had given up a meaningful job and a good income, not knowing if she would ever find anything comparable in LA. She had no friends in her new town and didn't know how to meet people.

Viviane had to tolerate the distance separating her from the people and things she loved. She had to cope with mixed perceptions of the new world where she now lived. She believed Los Angeles to be a dangerous place where she would have to be wary of carjacking, high-speed chases, muggings, and other dangers. Loneliness, fear, identity issues, social disorientation, and isolation are just a sampling of the difficulties my client suffered after moving to a new country.

My job was to coach her through the process of separating the practical issues from the emotional ones so she could tackle them one at a time. Practically, Viviane needed a new résumé, so we wrote one. She ably handled the everyday practical demands, so we took on the emotional aspects one by one. First, we developed a systematic plan to help fill some voids in her life. Although we couldn't replace her family and friends, we devised ways she could meet new people and build friendships with some.

My client was aware that, for a time, her emotional state would be intense, but in time, the sad and lonely feelings would subside, as she filled the empty spaces in her new life. As Viviane's story illustrates, a complex transition such as hers influences nearly every element of everyday life. Between her strength and determination and her husband's continuing support, she was eventually able to adjust. She found friends, landed a good job, and settled into her new world.

What the Gap Is and Isn't

Whereas change is inevitable, growth is optional. Transitions represent opportunities to stretch ourselves, so we can navigate our way safely and surely from the old world to the new. Like Viviane, the better we understand the feelings and experiences we might face in the Gap, the more prepared we'll be to deal the other side. To help that outcome, here are some misconceptions about the Gap as well as some of its common characteristics.

The Gap itself is not necessarily a dark place. In describing the difficulties and challenges of transitions, I might give the impression that the Gap is a negative place, and it's best to stay away from it. Having spent considerable time in the Gap, I perceive it as a place of learning, challenge, and growth, but let's be real. Transition follows change, and human nature being what it is, many of us resist change and do our best to avoid it. For example, think of the people who chronically complain about change while being stymied by it. Some have taken this dubious skill to an art form!

Some (perhaps many) transition periods are painful, such as grieving the loss of a job or a loved one, suffering a critical accident or illness, or severe financial setbacks. But when we step up to the plate and face our adversities head on, we stand close to a new life. Extreme events can inspire (or require) us to pause, reflect, and raise deep, pivotal questions, and consequently, we grow in ways we never expected. We transform because of the stormy place we were willing to enter and successfully navigate.

The Gap is a zone of change. Change is the starting point of a transition, and big changes can shake the foundations of our lives, attitudes, social status, self-image, perceptions, values, and occasionally, our beliefs. The Gap is where we weather the storm between our old world and the new, from ripples to waves to wild, unbridled turbulence. Not only does our world change, but we also change with it—from temporary discomfort and disorientation to (occasionally) complete transformation.

The Gap is where self-discovery and personal growth will occur if we allow the process to follow its natural course. For those blessed with a heightened sense of self-awareness, times of challenge might not be necessary for insight or enlightenment. For the rest of us, there are gifts to be found inside the Gap, insights and revelations we would not otherwise discover. Although our journey through the Gap might require struggle, indecision, or moments of self-doubt, we must face ourselves openly and squarely at a point in the process. For some, this might mean

> *It's important to distinguish change from transition.*

working through periods of anger, resentment, or other forms of suffering; these emotional aspects accompany every transition. As in twelve-step recovery programs, some of us will have to hit bottom before we encounter the epiphany that can and will propel us. This is a time to go inward, so we can take some deep, long looks at who we are and who we want to be. Here, we sort things and find some answers because we are willing to ask the hard questions. Some of us might seek the help of a therapist or spiritual advisor during this period to give us guidance, support, and sound advice.

The Gap doesn't always have a clear starting line. When there is a sudden, unexpected change in your life, you know exactly where and when your transition began, but that's not always the case. Take retirement, for example. If you are thinking about your retirement date, planning, preparing, or making adjustments in your old world—as it relates to the expected ending date of your career—then, indeed, you have begun the transition, whether you know it.

Some people so anticipate their long-awaited retirement that they either quit taking on big projects or stop putting forth their full effort, knowing an end is in sight. They let their minds slip into the future, like the old Eagles song, "I'm Already Gone." Others might get nostalgic about the past to put off having to think about their foggy future. People often bounce between yesterday and the tomorrow during transition periods.

While I'm on this topic, allow me to put on my coaching hat and take brief diversion. Particularly when it comes to retirement, I want to encourage you to become a "cattail" on your way out. When a cattail matures, it literally explodes (albeit mildly), thereby dispersing its soft seeds. When you retire (that is, mature), treat your knowledge and wisdom as your seeds, and on your way out, "explode" and disperse them, allowing them also to grow and mature. Okay, that's another book; let me get back on course.

In some cases, not only is the transition "starting line" unclear, but it also can get very "complicated" with certain transitions. For instance, adolescence offers a glimpse into what is seemingly a very natural process of transitioning, but which can be a very foggy gap both for the adolescent and the parent. During this phase—or transition—is a fair amount of conflict and tension, in part, because in each of their respective minds, the transition begins at different times.

The adolescent is ready to be independent, but the parent might not believe he or she is ready.

Sometimes, it's the other way around. The parent is all too ready for that child to leave, but the unmotivated son or daughter just hangs around. There is actually a third scenario. I recall when my son Kevin and his mother, with whom he was living, struggled with this situation. When he was about 19, they both had very mixed feelings about his going out on his own. On the one hand, they both knew it was time to move on, but because they had a very strong and loving bond, it was a struggle to "take the leap." He eventually moved out on his own, and as with any two people who love each other, the separation was challenging, but both did magnificently well in the end. Perhaps the distinctive lesson in this type of transition is, again, to recognize that the starting line is blurry, and it might come at different times for all involved.

It is not always clear where the Gap ends, or if indeed, it does. I lost my mother in 1975 (I was only sixteen), and her death was the beginning of my transition of learning to live without a mother. I still think of her, miss her, and wonder what life would have been like if she were alive. Adjusting to this loss was a long and difficult transition for me. The moment when this crucial life change began for me was clear and distinct, and I spent considerable time in the Gap, as I reluctantly let go of my old world and adapted to the new one. Yet I'm not sure my transition ended, or if it ever did. This phase might never completely end for me. I know things have changed for me through the years, but sometimes, I just don't believe that it's over.

Some people are stuck in the Gap, and they never fully make it to the new world. Depending on the person and the circumstances, the Gap can represent an intimidating, unnerving, or traumatic period. The ambiguity, uncertainty, and foggy nature of the Gap can cause some of us to withdraw or shield ourselves behind our mental and physical defenses for self-protection. Sadly, this causes us to shut down instead of open up to our "new normal." Some people are caught up in the Gap's whirlwind for years, much like a washer stuck in the spin cycle. You've been around some of these people; one of their laments is "if only…" They're held hostage by their inability to let go of the old world, stuck in a repetitive pattern like the movie Groundhog Day. This sometimes happens to a parent after a child's death. It's easy to comprehend the level of grief that accompanies this unthinkable loss, but sometimes, for years, so much attention is directed toward the dead child that the surviving siblings feel left in the cold. This dedication to prolonged suffering serves no one. Yes, it sounds like a cliché, but truly, life is for the living. We can keep our cherished memories alive, honor our lost loved ones, and still move on.

Change is inevitable; growth is optional.

Some people never complete their transitions because they choose to back off instead of push forward when they hit the pressure points in the Gap, forcing them to remain derailed, defenseless, and stuck. At best, their forward motion is minimal, not enough to reach the other side. I have empathy for those who cannot complete their journeys, because they miss so much potential.

Few of us are told while growing up that loss, adversity, or setbacks bring opportunity. I am here to assure you that the Gap is a natural and normal adjustment period following a significant change. It's not a place to fear, but one to face. Preparation, openness, honesty, perseverance, and empathetic support help you weather the storm, make it to the other side, and reap the benefits awaiting you.

Playing With Your Life Savings

An important point that I like to remember and want to point out here is the emotional pain of being lost, confused, and depressed was and can be so great at times. Who knows exactly why this happens to some and not others. In my case, I think in part it was because of the intensity of my plans—the years of thought and emotion I had invested toward this moment in time.

A good metaphor is investing money. Without working for it, if you luckily came across $1,000 and decided to invest it in the stock market, but then lost it all after several months, it would sting, but the grief would be little. But if you spent a lifetime saving and investing time, effort and money, and you lost it all, this would likely have a crushing effect on most. The challenge of transition often depends on the conditions and investment preceding the change. Perhaps I didn't consider this well enough, but it's an important question and issue to deliberate. You must consider "what if you fail?"

Summary of "A Glimpse Inside the Gap":

- The level of your openness and willingness to persevere and embrace or internalize your lessons will determine how much you (and your life) transform.
- Every new experience comes with its set of emotional, social, or physical aspects.
- Loss is a built-in component of a transition.
- The more time a person has spent in the old world, the harder the transition can be.
- The less familiar we are with the new world awaiting us the more turbulent our Gap will be.
- It's important to distinguish change from transition.
- The early stages of transitions involve facing a series of practical, doable tasks often complicated by emotional issues.
- Change is inevitable; growth is optional.
- The Gap itself is not necessarily a dark place.
- The Gap is a zone of change.
- The Gap is where self-discovery and personal growth will occur if we allow the process to follow its natural course.
- The Gap doesn't always have a clear starting line.
- It is not always clear where the Gap ends, or if indeed, it does.
- Some people are stuck in the Gap, and they never fully make it to the new world.

Personal Reflections:

1. Think of a major change that occurred in your life.

   - What were the emotional, social, and physical aspects of the change?
   - What were the positive aspects of the change? What were the challenging aspects?
   - Did you feel the need to move quickly through the transition, or did you take your time?

2. Do you believe the Gap is a place to learn and grow? [Specifically] how did you learn and grow in your last transition? How can you use that wisdom going forward?

3. Are you going through a change, or is a change in your future?

   - What losses will you experience because of the change (tangible and intangible)?
   - Which losses will you find most difficult to deal with?
   - Can those losses be replaced? If yes, with what or how can you do so?
   - If they can't be replaced, how will you cope to move forward?

Chapter 3

How the Gap Can Sneak up on Us

When some friends sent their last child off to college, the mother found this transition especially difficult. It wasn't that she merely missed her youngest child, she was also confronted with a potentially life-altering question: *Who am I now that I have lost my active mothering role and no longer have a child at home?* For more than two decades, Jill had been a dedicated full-time mother, but now she felt a huge void in her life. Jill had been so wrapped up in the role and tasks of motherhood she had never felt the need or desire to define herself in any other context. But she now faced a dramatic change that would redefine her role and purpose in life.

Jill had indeed expected an adjustment period involving some void, but as many of us do when facing something new and uncomfortable, she tried not to think too much about this great change in her life. Her days felt long and empty, but she thought this was normal, and eventually, the feeling would pass.

Sometimes, she and her husband would enjoy second-honeymoon moments, but these were infrequent. Over time, the emptiness in her life turned to apathy, and her lack of purpose lapsed into depression. As Jill began to ask questions about the rest of her life, she realized there were no easy answers. Soon, her marriage became strained because she and her husband had been so focused on their parenting roles they'd forgotten how to be partners. They were lost. They didn't know what to do.

You can probably sense that not one problem, but a series, had driven this unsuspecting couple into a foggy Gap. The obvious issue, of course, was the difficulty they were having as empty nesters. Because their parenthood and provider roles had taken precedence over their marital partnership, they now had little to share intimately. They still cared for each other, but over time, as it happens with many couples, their relationship had shifted from that of lovers to parenting partners. They had little to sustain them as a couple, other than their identity as parents. They were in a holding pattern, feeling distant and unconnected, unsure what to do next.

You've had your transition periods, so you know that we often back into change and transition without realizing we are embedded in a new situation that took us off guard. Just as the wheels of a car slowly sink and get embedded in deep mud, you often don't realize what's happening until it's too late. You veered into the slipstream of the Gap without realizing it and cruised past the point of no return before you could back up or back off.

The Slipstream of the Gap

Realization that you're poised between the old world and the new one often doesn't occur until you've tackled some practical issues connected to your transition. Your attention is so focused on your to do list that it feels impossible to look too far ahead. Then, reality sets in, and the emotional elements begin to mount, which is what happened with my client Viviane. Only after the physical elements of her move had been addressed did Viviane begin to realize how lonely and sad she felt.

It's common to feel let down, lost, or adrift once we have handled the excitement or preoccupation with the physical elements of a change. It's a bit like getting lost on a hike; you stride along and then realize you're no longer on the main trail. You don't know when or where you veered off course, but you're not where you want to be. You start to feel anxious, disoriented, and maybe immobilized. You have no idea where you are or which way to go, so you stay

> *Discomfort and disorientation are normal responses to navigating through uncharted territory.*

where you are, hoping for a revelation, rescue, or divine intervention. Until you've made your next decision, you are hovering ungrounded in unfamiliar territory.

This sounds frightening and dramatic, and it is. The feelings are real. It helps to realize, though, that discomfort and disorientation are natural and normal responses to navigating through uncharted territory. Sometimes, we can find our way alone. Other times, we lack the means to get back on track, rethink our situation, or figure out a new direction without help. What makes the difference is how long we allow ourselves to be immobilized, if we have the commitment or determination to forge ahead despite the unknowns, and whether we are willing to ask for guidance or outside intervention to help us find our way.

In the Middle of the Muddle

Growing up in North Carolina, I loved playing in the woods. One day, while feeling high on confidence and low in caution, I came across a large sewage pipe straddling a deep, wide, dry gully. The pipe was perhaps 30 feet long and high up the bank on the far side, but where I stood, it lay close to the ground. I decided to cross the chasm by belly crawling along the pipe. At first, it was fun and adventurous—I felt like Indiana Jones.

But before I reached the halfway point, I realized this wasn't going to be as easy as I expected. Then, I looked down and reality set in—I was already at least 20 feet above the ground, and there were piles of boulders in the draw below.

I looked back and then ahead, calculating the distance to the end of the pipe. It was a long way off. "Okay"—I thought to myself—"the fun now gone." I tried to stay calm so I could figure my way out of this pickle. Maybe I could just turn back. But because I was straddling the pipe, turning around or even backing up seemed riskier than going forward. Panic set in. I was petrified, unable to move forward or backward. So I just lay there, frozen in place, holding my breath, wondering how I had gotten myself into such a mess, afraid I would never get out of it.

I survived my childhood misadventure, but what I experienced parallels what happens when we come face to face with a transition so complex that it can't be traversed in one felled swoop (or even a few). Little did I know, at my tender age, that this was my introduction to the Gap. Similar to my perilous pipe crawl, there comes the moment in real life when we realize how uncomfortable we are and how precarious we feel, but we know we can't possibly go back; we can only move forward.

Once you realize you have passed the Gap's threshold, you recognize that you've entered a zone of reckoning where you feel yourself suspended between the old world and the new. There, you hover, perhaps as unhinged as I was, desperately clinging to that big pipe perched above the rocks. Despite the panic, my instincts screamed, "Think. Don't be foolish!" We all know intuitively that hysterically forging headlong into a threatening or unknown situation is foolhardy and fraught with potential perils and problems. But so is blindly bolting back to where we came from. That's the tricky nature of the Gap.

The bad news is that realistically, your old world, as you knew it, no longer exists. You can't hang on to the status quo even if you want to. At this point, even if you returned to your old world, there would be losses of some sort because things have already changed. That's an inherent quality of transition. Once you reach the Gap, things can never go back the way they were, however much you hope or wish. Something or someone will be different somehow, including you. That's why you must move forward. If you've ever had a chance to revisit a Friday night football game—at your former high school from which you graduated only a year earlier—you know that, despite many of your friends still being in high school, you don't fit in any longer. Your worlds have changed, and you can't go back to the old one.

Being Stuck in the Gap

Some people get so intimidated at the thought of moving on (or they romanticize a less-than-perfect) that they allow themselves to be stuck in the Gap's slipstream for years. Mind you, this is not a safe place. I define being stuck as being in *fixed emotional disorientation ranging from moderate to extreme.* Extended inaction fosters feelings of inadequacy and impotence, expressed by self-punishing emotions such as frustration, blame, helplessness, or hopelessness. Some victims numb themselves with food or substance abuse to avoid self-confrontation.

This sad state of affairs is a waste of human potential because these people give up their power. They choose to be bitter rather than working to make their lives better. They allow themselves to live in continuous postponement like an airplane stuck in an interminable holding pattern because of bad weather. For some people, this goes on for years, maybe even decades. Think of the waste! Although I don't believe that anyone should rush to judgment or act without deliberate thought, my heart goes out to those who make the Gap their permanent home.

Being Stuck Can Sometimes Be the Answer

Although this might sound contradictory, being stuck isn't always undesirable. Even though it might not feel like it, being temporarily stopped (or stymied) can be what you need. You have time to reflect and ponder your situation rather than letting panic or fear take over. The last thing you want to do is impulsively try to escape your dilemma without careful thought and planning.

Sometimes, being stuck in the slipstream is *exactly* the wake-up call you needed to shift your perspective, giving you a chance to see life differently. You might take time to evaluate where you are and what you need to go next, so you can decide to move on. Being stuck can force you to spend some time looking inward instead of focusing on outside circumstances. You can do some serious reflection; you can ask (and answer) important questions about your values, priorities, and the direction you want your life to take. Perhaps you know the phrase, "where there is darkness, you must shine the light." Occasionally, being stuck supplies that beam of enlightenment you were searching for because you're dormant instead of driven by action. You have to be in an open receptive state before you can truly clear your mind and calmly think through things.

At some point in your life, you've probably heard someone say, "And then I hit rock bottom." Although this phrase is often used when referring to an alcohol or drug addiction, we've all had those moments when we had to own up, take stock, and squarely face ourselves. Some people call this "the dark night of the soul." For some, hitting bottom is necessary because the person is forced to realize there is nowhere else to go; they will be stuck in the spin cycle indefinitely until they act. For you, being temporarily stuck might not mean to hit bottom, but a catalyst that sparks urgency, introspection, critical thinking, and a desire to improve the situation.

As an impetuous boy, in facing my first transition from safety to danger and back again, I lacked the experience and maturity to understand any of this. Instead of getting panicky and exposing myself to serious injury, I let myself stay stuck awhile. I held fast to that pipe, crying every tear I could muster and praying every word I knew. I promised the Lord I'd never do anything like that again if only I could escape the predicament. After lying still long enough for boyish restlessness and boredom to replace my fear, I slowly and carefully began to slither and squirm toward the pipe's far side. There was only one thought in mind: get to the end! I had slain my dragon of fear (or as I like to call it, the emotional "drag on"), a life lesson we all need to learn despite age.

Sometimes, being stuck is exactly the wake-up call needed to shift your perspective.

Reeling with Feeling

The hardest transitions are forced on us. Being fired from a job, discovering a spouse's infidelity, and surviving a loved one's death are among the toughest adjustments we must make in life. The inability to go back to the old world, even if you wanted to, compounds the intensity of forced transitions. Like the lobster that loses its shell so it can grow a new one, you must remain vulnerable for a time. Change has happened, and you can't stop it. Your old world has become part of your past. You can only go forward, even though you might be unsure you have the strength or tenacity to do it. As you fight for equilibrium and answers, you hover in the Gap between two worlds, gathering strength, insight, and endurance.

It's common that once we realize we've entered the transition zone, or the Gap, our first wish might be to turn back. We might dream of sneaking back toward the old familiar world, even if it wasn't so great; "It isn't much, but it's mine." After the breakup of the Soviet Union, I read an article about the many Russian citizens who wished to return to the Communist lifestyle and dictatorial government despite its limitations because democracy was so foreign, uncomfortable, and difficult. The freedom and opportunities offered by a freer lifestyle paled in comparison to the comfort of how things used to be.

All transitions trigger a complex upwelling of emotion. Feelings can include fear, panic, discomfort, resistance, anger, sadness, blame, excitement, elation, happiness, joy, or pleasure. The emotions you feel depend on the transition, the circumstances of the old world, the promise or threat of the new world, your state of mind and body, and the extent of your coping skills. The more mentally hardy you are the more inner reserves you will have to draw on, and the combination of preparation and determination will give you the stamina you need to go on.

The Gap ... For the Grieving
A few years ago, a friend suffered the sudden death of her husband. They shared a close, loving relationship while raising three beautiful children. I remember sitting through the funeral service feeling

a deep despair for Amy and her children. I couldn't stop thinking about how difficult it would be for them to survive the coming year and beyond. I thought about all the holidays and special family events that would intensify her despair and grief, especially during that first year. I remember the first Christmas after Tom's death. Considering how this season brings out deep emotions, my heart was heavy as I thought about Amy and her children and the difficulty of the holidays without Tom. Then, I read this touching letter she wrote in an annual booklet produced by our church.

Count Your Blessings
Thursday, December 20, 2007

When I was invited to write this reflection about what Christmas and the Advent season meant to me, I had to really stop and think. Losing Tom this year, my soul mate, has forced me to change my actions and my way of thinking from the norm.

My first reaction was that Christmas is not going to be the same. It is going to be very different this year for me, my kids, and my whole family. How can we even celebrate this Christmas with the same meaning as before? How am I going to even celebrate at all without my husband and father of our children? The mere thought of this has made my stomach and heart truly ache.

But after thinking it over, the answer was very clear and easy. I was going to be strong and just do it. The Grinch was not going to get away with stealing our Christmas. Whether I wanted to ignore the holidays this year or not, they were still going to happen. Advent means "to come" or "the period before the celebration of the birth of Jesus Christ." Even though celebrating Christmas will be difficult without Tom, he will be my inspiration to do so. In a letter he wrote to family and friends back in 2005, he stressed that even in our hectic lives we should remember the many blessings that we have been given. My approach this Advent will be to focus on what I do have: my children, family and friends, my church, the memories of a relationship with the most wonderful man one could ask for, and most of all, my strong belief in God and Jesus Christ.

As this assignment has challenged me to face what could easily have been an unbearable season, I am still grateful for the opportunity to share my thoughts. Though difficult, it has made me stop and think about the true meaning of Christmas and all the many blessings I have been given.

I will end my reflection with a quote from the letter that Tom wrote: As a final thought, each of you has been blessed in similar ways that I have been. Don 't make the same mistake that I have made in the past by taking things for granted. It is my hope that you will 'stop and smell the roses' because they are blooming all around you.

I invite you, too, this year, to join me in "Counting Our Blessings" for they are all around us!

Merry Christmas,
Amy L. Nance

Clearly, Amy will not allow circumstance to dictate what she will feel or how she will live her life. Surely, she grieved for Tom, and she misses him very much. But she also understands that she can choose her attitude, which will help her be more in control of her transition. Think of the beautiful, self-empowering lesson she is passing along to her children.

Although she will grieve, Amy is clear on her intention to learn and grow, emotionally and spiritually. Thanks to her depth of self and spiritual awareness, she not only prevailed during this difficult transition, but she likely will also discover new dimensions in herself and so will each of her children.

We all can prevail over adversity, and it starts with recognizing that we always can choose our attitude. Let me emphasize that, despite the intensity of your transition or circumstance, your attitude is your choice. Keep this in mind as you face your transitions.

No Easy Way Out

Many of us have a secret fantasy of winning the lottery, figuring this welcome life transition would instantly solve most of our problems. But if you read the stories of the big winners, most admit that the initial thrill and excitement are soon replaced with a huge sense of letdown. Reality sets in as close relationships and lifestyle make big shifts. It doesn't take long for the Gap to impose itself on the scene. The new millionaires, without the help of a set of lifelines are now hit with serious and unexpected issues and questions that are a major challenge to answer.

"What do I really want to do with my life now that I have money?"
"Now that I have everything I want, why am I not happier?"
"Will my friends and family still love me for who I am, or are they only after my money?"
"Is this all there is? What comes next?"

"I thought having money would change my life, but do I really feel different inside?"

The confusion and disappointment can be crippling. The trouble is that instant millionaires are still who they were before they "struck gold." If they didn't have their act together before the windfall, they won't be blessed with instant enlightenment or a wealth of insight. When anyone is confronted by life's deep, searching questions, and they let them go unanswered, these unfortunate people pave their road to Stuckville, despite how much money they do or don't have.

Another excellent book by Marshall Goldsmith, "What Got You Here Won't Get You There," offers a good point to think about when it comes to traversing the Gap. While his book addresses leadership development, the title itself can be applied to life transitions. It is inside the Gap where you can substantially learn and grow and take things to another level. However, you must also recognize that what got you in the Gap—be it luck, bad habits, or your good looks—won't necessarily get you successfully through the Gap or to the next level. You have to discover what it takes, and the discovery comes from asking good questions—the right questions.

> *Being temporarily stuck can be the catalyst that sparks urgency, introspection, critical thinking, and a desire to improve the situation.*

Avoidance often leads to more conflict, triggering emotions that might range from mild anxiety to panic and desperation. When we fear or resist answering life's hard questions, we increase the chances of being stuck in the middle of our muddle. When we're stuck in the Gap, making our way toward the new world pales in comparison to escaping the emotional turmoil we fear and loathe. Author C. Leslie Charles says, "When we act out of fear, we end up creating the very outcome we were trying to avoid." Perhaps you can relate; I can. The hardest part to grasp in this complicated process is that those threatening, fearsome questions that make us squirm in the answering tap into our innate wisdom if we have the courage to tackle them. Go figure!

Summary of
"How the Gap Can Sneak up on Us":

- We often back into change and transition without realizing we are embedded in a new situation that took us off guard.
- It's common to feel let down, lost, or adrift once we have handled the excitement or preoccupation with the physical [and practical] elements of a change.
- Discomfort and disorientation are natural and normal responses to navigating through uncharted territory.
- There comes the moment in real life when we realize how uncomfortable we are and how precarious we feel (in the Gap), but we know we can't possibly go back; we can only move forward.
- Once you reach the Gap, things can never go back the way they were. Something or someone will be different somehow, including you. You must move forward.
- Being "stuck" is being in fixed emotional disorientation ranging from moderate to extreme.
- Sometimes, being stuck is exactly the wake-up call you needed to shift your perspective—a chance to see life differently.
- Being temporarily stuck can be a catalyst that sparks urgency, introspection, critical thinking, and a desire to improve the situation.
- If you're stuck, and you get into a spin cycle, you will be there until you act.
- The hardest transitions are the ones forced on us.
- Once we enter a (difficult) Gap, often, our first thought is to turn back.
- Transitions trigger a complex upwelling of emotion. The more mentally hardy you are, the more inner reserves you will have to draw on.
- We can prevail over adversity, and it starts by choosing our attitude.
- When confronted by life's deep, searching questions, if we let them go unanswered, we pave our road to Stuckville.

Personal Reflections:

1. Some aspects of our world define us.

   - What aspects of your world define you?
   - Are you able and willing to redefine yourself when those aspects change, or do you hang back in the old world, fighting to hold on to the old definition of yourself?

2. Is your "life purpose" carved in stone, or does it evolve as your "roles" change?

3. Do you deal effectively with situations that cause negative feelings (frustration, anger, and so on)? What coping skills could you develop to handle those situations more effectively?

4. Are you stuck in the Gap?

   - If you believe you are "stuck," reevaluate and determine if you are actually stuck versus moving slowly.
   - What do you need to do to move forward?

Chapter 4

The Connection Between
Transitions and Time

Our busy, bustling culture doesn't exactly support the idea of spending much time working on life's hard questions or even slowly picking your way through a difficult transition. Like a speed date, it's expected that you'll take the express lane through crisis or change so you can hurry and get to the other side. It's assumed, as Bruce Springsteen sang, that we were "born to run." Rather than spending long periods of inactivity, introspection, or going inside ourselves, society expects us to keep moving, even if we have no idea where we're going.

Busy is the watchword of the day, and productivity is the norm. Consider how often a friend might greet you with a, "Hi, how have you been—busy?" as if it's a good thing (or the only thing). In our society, we are expected to live in a flurry of constant "productivity," though no one defines it. Isn't *thinking* productive? If you want to derail a conversation, the next time someone asks what you've been up to, tell the person you've been *thinking*. Chances are they'll look at you as if you said "you were just visited by aliens."

Chronically hustling and bustling keeps us preoccupied and distracted instead of self-aware and sensitive to our environment. In our "full steam ahead" society, we seldom have the time, nor do we take the time, to stop and think about how today's actions position us for tomorrow. This is the challenge (and blessing) of major life transitions; they often force us to spend time in that rare place of contemplation and soul searching where we can consciously and conscientiously reflect on our lives and our issues.

A transition can bring with it a time of isolation and self-analysis that requires addressing crucial questions such as:

Who am I?

What do I want in life?

If I keep doing what I'm doing, will that take me where I want to be?

What are my goals, values, beliefs, and priorities?

Am I living in alignment with my values, beliefs, and priorities?

What do I need to do, not do, or do differently to enhance who I am as a person?

What important issues am I avoiding or refusing to address?

What might happen if I start to tend to these issues?

What might happen if I don't?

Am I prepared for the outcomes either way?

So many of us consciously or unconsciously exist in such an extreme state of preoccupation and distraction we never have the time or mental space to think about these important matters, much less deal with them proactively.

Because of our chronic busyness, we end up reacting to the (false) urgency of trivia and low-level daily demands instead of focusing on our core values. *In The 7 Habits of Highly Effective People*, Stephen Covey contends that if you spend your life on the "important" items rather than the merely "urgent," you can avoid many major crises. Consider those who say their family is a major priority, but they spend little time and energy in family involvement. The same principle applies to health mainte-nance issues. True to human nature, we might say one thing but do another as we put off what we know is important, but not urgent, which is how some of us find ourselves alone, unnerved, and adrift in the slipstream of the Gap.

> *The blessing and challenge of major life transitions; they force us to spend time in that rare place of contemplation and soul searching.*

The Only Time You Have Is Now

You probably know people who cling to the past and long for the good old days or those who constantly worry about the future as if their hand-wringing or tooth-grinding will stop anything bad from happening. Yet, the only time we can truly control is now. My wife Jane has taught me about the value of being "present," more in the moment. Thanks to her, I have more awareness about how I spend my time and the discipline to resist keeping myself stuck in chronic busyness or preoccupation.

Thanks to Jane's counsel, not only do I take the time to be with my loved ones so we can spend precious time together, but I also allow myself occasions of solitude. During my alone time, I analyze my thoughts and actions and where they are directing me. I also evaluate how I feel about where I'm going. If I don't like the answers I uncover, I alter my thought process and change my actions.

Thanks to our hurry-up culture, many of us live our lives at warp speed with little time dedicated to reflecting on our daily experiences. We barely have time to scrutinize what we did in a given day and why, much less take the time to consider what matters most and whether our actions match our priorities. Perhaps like the rest of us, you've had moments when you thought your life was spinning out of control. If so, please know that this is nature's way of telling you to slow down and smell the coffee before the pot burns dry.

> *Values and priorities slip into the background when we consistently let the urgent override the important.*

Daily, I see people rushing about, hurrying through their lives. They don't realize how many of their daily activities are driven by the external demands: work, long commutes, family matters, school, personal and social obligations, church activities, and more. Add a hobby or sport if it can be crammed in with everything else, and each day becomes little more than an exercise in doing as much as you can. Workdays, weekends, or even those long-awaited vacations become a timed event. We all need to recognize a connection between the overloaded lifestyle and being derailed by life's unanticipated emergencies. Values and priorities slip into the background when we consistently let the urgent override the important.

Here is my definition of the distracted, preoccupied, busy-bee lifestyle:

- It's the insidious exercise of assuming everything must be done while overestimating your ability to do it all.

50

- It's being unaware or oblivious of the time you waste in nonessential activities.
- It's a disorderly multitasking mental state in which you limit your imagination and creativity.
- It's a subtle dream killer that keeps you so mired in a comfort zone of unquestioned activity that you don't have time to visualize alternate outcomes for you or your family.
- It's a convenient escape mechanism that creates a bogus sense of satisfaction and productivity.
- It's a way of life based on short-term distractions instead of long-term dreams.

Living in overload mode functions as a barrier to identifying your true self and the values you hold dear. It prevents you from clarifying what's most important in your life and keeps you from confronting your fears, embracing change, staying motivated, and engaging in positive actions that align with your priorities.

Stop, Look, Listen

So what am I suggesting? Self-awareness is the pathway to personal fulfillment. When we stay tuned in to what we do and why, we become—and remain—an active player in our lives. We don't fall prey to the social pressures telling us who we are supposed to be and what kind of lifestyle we should have. Slowing down and taking time to examine our thoughts and actions provides the opportunity to identify patterns of behavior that could prevent us from living life as fully as we would like. We might also discover how we bring joy and love into our lives. Think of the advantages of doing this kind of introspection as preventive maintenance; that is, you stop and reflect because you want to, not because you must, because by then, it's often too late.

If you're unaccustomed to in-depth exploration, you might initially feel a bit uncomfortable or perhaps even a little silly. But it's necessary if you want to know yourself better and an essential exercise if you want to free yourself of unrealistic expectations, external obligations, and trivial activities that draw you away from your goals. For some people, crisis or forced change can be the best thing that ever happened to them because it was their moment of reckoning or hitting bottom. For the first time in a long time (or perhaps ever), they had to stop running and start to ask important questions that would draw them to the core of what's important in their lives. Questions such as these are helpful to ask and answer:

- What or who do I consider most important in my life?
- How do my daily activities support (or contradict) this importance?
- What behavior changes on my part would improve my lifestyle, health, or state of relationships?
- In reviewing, what is the biggest lesson I've learned so far and how am I putting this wisdom into practice daily?
- If I continue going in the same direction I've been headed, what will be the most likely outcome?
- How do I feel about that?
- What do I truly want to happen, and how can I achieve this?
- What is my first step, and how will I encourage myself to go on?

Working through these kinds of questions isn't easy, but it's imperative if you want to continue your development as a human being. Finding the answers requires reflection, deep introspection, and most of all, brutal honesty. As it is said, "To thine own self be true." Although the truth is sometimes difficult to face, this is also your opportunity to redefine who you are and what you're all about.

Defining Moments

In any life-altering transition exists the possibility of insights so profound that they change your life for good. You have a revelation and see things as you never did; you decide and act on it. In other words, you step up to the plate. This is called a defining moment. One potential turnaround moment is the feeling of shock and unease when you realize that things aren't going the way you had hoped, expected, or dreamed. Another is the moment of reckoning when circumstances force you to stop in your tracks and face reality. That's when, out of necessity, you quit being preoccupied

In any life altering transition exists the possibility of insights so profound that they change your life for good.

or distracted and go inside to figure things out. You can probably identify a few of your defining moments and how you took charge and changed your circumstances because you changed yourself.

When you take on those deep, searching, and occasionally painful questions about the state of your life and your being, you force yourself to be in the moment. You are truly taking charge of your life. This is a gift that comes with transition—the opportunity to get back on track, or a pivotal point to take your life in a new direction or to another level. I urge you to take the time to know yourself better, to make the crucial link between your daily activities and their systematically shaping of your future. The more conscious and consistent you are in making this process a daily practice, the better your chances of steering clear of the Gap. At the least, you'll minimize the possibility of being stuck, and what a time-saver that will be.

Summary of
"The Connection Between Transitions and Time":

- Our busy society assumes and sometimes expects us to move quickly through the Gap.
- Chronically hustling and bustling keeps us preoccupied and distracted instead of aware.
- Particularly during a transition, it is necessary to slow down (in mind, body, and spirit) and be introspective; so we can learn and grow.
- The blessing *and challenge* of major life transitions; they force us to spend time in that rare place of contemplation and soul-searching.
- Take time to analyze your thoughts and actions and where they are directing you. If you don't like the answers you uncover, change your thoughts and actions.
- Values and priorities slip into the background when we consistently let the urgent override the important.
- Self-awareness is a part of the pathway to personal fulfillment.
- To thine own self be true.
- In any life-altering transition exists the possibility of insights so profound that they change your life for good.

Personal Reflections:

1. Slow down for a moment and reflect on a few questions posed in this chapter.
   - What really matters to you in your life—and do your actions match your priorities?
   - What do you want in or out of life?
   - Ideally, if you could re-create your life, what would it look like?
   - If you keep doing what you're doing, will that take you where you want to be?

2. What did you learn, or are you learning, from being in the Gap?

3. External demands and obligations often prevent us from living a life of our choosing.
   - What external demands and obligations are driving your time and life?
   - What can you let go of that will give you more time to live a proactive life—one that you choose?
   - What steps can you take to take control of your time and your life?

4. What truths about yourself must you face before you can move forward? (Examples: "I'm afraid I might not be unable to make it alone.)

Chapter 5

From Dreaming to Doing

We often describe life as a journey with its highways and byways, occasional detours and scenic loops, and this applies to change, transitions, or challenges we might face. But of course, life is more complex and unpredictable than any road trip could ever be. Consider that, despite our lofty goals, whenever change presents, we operate without a map. Think about the times you've had to make your way through the hazy unknown circumstances changed or shifted on you, which is why the Gap's fog zone is so disorienting. No maps or posted signs tell us which way we should head or where we need to turn.

Sometimes, a transition is so sudden or so abrupt that you feel as if you were dropped into the middle of a vast and barren land without a clue to where you are or where you need to go, but here's the good news. If we are willing to stop, look, and listen, there are a few signs along our troubled road. It might be a dim memory from our past, remnants of a conversation from long ago, or a vague sense of familiarity, as if we've passed this spot before. We might gain insight from something we read, or a friend might make a passing statement too profound to dismiss. There might be a sudden revelation, an "aha!" moment that seems to flash from nowhere.

Signs and messages of hope come from all kinds of unexpected sources. Your subconscious mind might even go to work for you and deliver its message as a dream; that's what happened to me. During my transition, I had an unforgettable dream that ended up being some inspiration for this book.

Viva Las Vegas

In my dream, I was driving to Las Vegas. The road was unfamiliar, but I felt relaxed and confident because I had a good map, and the highway was well marked. Suddenly, I found myself out of my car standing in the middle of the wide-open desert. There were no roads, no other vehicles, and no landmarks, just a huge void.

I stood frozen in place. I had no idea where to turn, and my instinct to stay put seemed more prudent than taking off in what might be the wrong direction. It was terrifying to feel so disoriented and so alone. I realized that I'd only have one shot at surviving a long trek across this boundless, dry desert. If I went the wrong way, it would surely be all over. So whatever decision I made, it *had* to be the right one the first time out. This notion almost paralyzed me. I stood there, confused and petrified, praying to God for a sign.

At some point in my dream, a gentle woman appeared, saying in a soft voice, "Kevin, I know you are heading to Las Vegas. It's that way. I'd be happy to go with you if you'd allow me to do so." I was skeptical, but I had no alternatives, so I asked, "Who are you, and how do you know where I'm going?" On the one hand, I wanted to trust her, but I didn't want to be hasty or naive.

It was getting dark, so I reluctantly agreed to let her guide me. We walked for hours, and I repeatedly asked her, "Are you sure this is the way? She assured me that it was, "telling me to have faith. I retorted, "Yeah? Well, I'll believe it when I see it." With a gentle firmness, she replied, "Kevin, sometimes, you have to *believe* it before you can see it."

We kept walking. Although there was no proof we were headed in the right direction, I felt a little better because at least I was going somewhere. I had a mission. It felt as if we walked for days, yet the surroundings didn't change, and this made me very nervous. I wondered if perhaps I should go back to where we started, but

Signs and messages of hope come from all kinds of unexpected sources. Pay attention.

then I'd dispel those doubts and continue to follow my guide, thinking what choice did I have. After all, she was kind, seemed confident, and didn't judge me for having lost my way. I began to trust her.

Suddenly, through the darkness, I thought I could detect a faint, blurry light in the distant sky. Perhaps just a mirage, but could that be city lights? I looked at my guide, and she said, "Yes, Kevin, that's Las Vegas. Let's keep walking." Though I wasn't convinced, I felt a tingle of confidence. If indeed this was Vegas, while still a long way off, it offered a ray of hope. Hope was what I desperately needed, and I felt a little better.

Daylight came, and we walked. Under the bright sun and blue sky, I could no longer see any lights, and again, I began to doubt myself.

Was Las Vegas there, or had I imagined it? My guide affirmed that we had seen the lights and that I needed faith and to keep my trust for just a bit longer.

As time wore on, I could see something in the distance. Though I couldn't make it out, I wanted to believe it was Las Vegas. My guide, realizing my anxiety, smiled and said, "Yes, Kevin, there it is." The closer we got, the clearer the city became. Finally, I could say with confidence, "Viva Las Vegas!" No longer was there a question of *whether* we would arrive, but only when. My destination lay before me; I was safe.

I don't know whether you've ever had a dream that brought you the answers you were looking for; this was a first for me. Perhaps your insights usually come in other form. Despite how they are packaged, I'm convinced that the answers we seek come to us if we're willing to lay self-doubt aside and pursue them. I mean that the answers are there for the asking. The answers we need lie deep inside us, which is why questions are so important. Questions turn us toward our inner wisdom.

Sometimes, I wonder about the course my life might have taken had my subconscious mind not intervened during my crisis, allowing my inner wisdom to guide me toward the answers for which I was looking.

My Las Vegas Lessons

1. Jump and the Net Will Appear

My friend Robin Crow wrote an excellent book called *Jump and the Net Will Appear*. In it, he suggests that there are times in life that you must take a leap of faith. Sometimes, that means having faith in you, faith in somebody else, or in my case, faith in God. When you are stuck in the Gap and struggle to get through the fog, taking a small leap of faith can be exactly what you need to get moving again. I'm not suggesting that you engage in irrational decisions or impulsive acts; your actions need to be deliberate. I'm also not suggesting that you will feel completely confident in whatever direction you take.

You will have doubts when facing the unknown, and yes, you will wonder if you're truly headed in the right direction, but at some point, you must make your move, which often involves a leap of faith. Trust yourself. Trust your knowledge, experience, wisdom, and intuition. Learn to trust your best instincts and have faith in the people who love and care about you. Take a step, make a move, and begin the process of getting through the fog.

2. Keep Moving

There's a saying, "Inch by inch, life's a cinch. Yard by yard, it's hard." When you begin to feel stuck or immobilized, the best antidote is positive action. Encourage yourself to take some step that will move you forward (or even sideways), even if it's only a small, slow, or cautionary step. The secret is to keep on keeping on. Taking positive steps might involve talking with someone you trust, reading a book, journaling your experiences, attending

Sometimes you have to believe it, to see it.

a workshop or seminar, or researching choices on the Internet. This action keeps you from feeling paralyzed, helpless, or hopeless.

It feels good to make some progress, even if it's slow and small. In time, you gain some momentum, which will boost your self-confidence. If you feel as if you're stuck, go back to those difficult, probing questions that will help shed some light on your situation. Be as honest as you can, and you'll discover inner wisdom you didn't know you had. Earlier in the book, I described what a helpless feeling it is to be immobilized. Perhaps you don't have complete confidence that you're moving in the right direction, but you'll find comfort in doing something rather than standing still. Do what you can to keep your bearings as you move forward, in case you need to adjust your course.

3. Find Someone You Can Trust

If you are stuck in the Gap, find a guide to help you through the vast unknown. It's important to work with someone you can trust. If you can afford it, hire the help. Short-term work with a coach or therapist could ease the most difficult part of your transition and give you the insights you need to take your next steps.

Your guide—whether your faith, spouse, a knowledgeable friend, counselor, or spiritual advisor—becomes the centerpiece of your trust. The guide you choose will be your supporter and challenger. He or she can help you clarify and organize your chaotic mental state. Your personal or professional guide can offer hope, common sense, a listening ear, and counsel to help you head out of that looming, wide-open desert and onto solid ground.

4. Believe in Yourself and Your Ability to Get Through the Gap

When you go through a major transition, your once-familiar environment shifts and changes, and you find yourself in unknown territory. Having no familiar landmarks is disorienting. Expect to experience conflicting emotions during this period, and do what you can to stay as centered and calm as possible. Resist overwhelming yourself with self-doubt, confusion, or fear to avoid being stuck. During any difficult or conflicting period, you might find it hard to trust your feelings or perceptions, but just as you allow yourself to have faith in someone else's wisdom, maintain faith in yourself. Believe in your skills, talents, experiences, and abilities. Your inner resources have helped you get this far in your life's journey, so have faith with all your heart that you have what it takes to get you through this challenging time, because you do.

The fog of self-doubt makes it difficult to see a problem objectively, complicating the process of finding workable choices and solutions. Without good decision making, the future remains blurry, like my vague, nighttime image of Las Vegas. There's much work to be done when you're trekking through the Gap, and you need self-confidence to take that first step and the ones that follow. Don't give up; keep going. Just as I did in my dream, I urge you to have or develop the faith you need to keep moving toward the light.

I often tell the story of my "desert dream" in my speeches and programs, and afterward, people will say, "That's exactly what I felt . . ." or "That's how I'm feeling right now." Repeatedly, people say, "It's as if someone dropped me into the middle of a wide-open desert with no idea about which way to go. I'm standing there, stopped by fear and confusion, unable to take even the first step because I'm clueless about where to go. I keep wondering what will happen if I choose a wrong direction, or even how I'll know I'm not going the right way."

A journey begins with the first step.

The Gap is real. It's a universal experience. You've traversed the vast expanse of the Gap in your life, found your way through the fog, and maybe you didn't even realize what a feat you achieved. Chances are you'll face the Gap again. The good news is that you don't have to be brought to a standstill and remain stuck or caught up in a frenzy of fear. You can find your way through the Gap if you are willing to keep your wits about you, take some risks, ask and answer good questions, and internalize the lessons you learn along the way. You've done it before, and you can do it again. Viva you!

Summary of "From Dreaming to Doing":

- A transition can be described as a road journey with its highways, byways, and occasional detours. Sometimes, we get lost.
- Signs and messages of hope come from all kinds of unexpected sources. Pay attention.
- Sometimes, you must believe it to see it. This is called faith.
- The answers we seek (in life) will come to us if we pursue them.
- Questions turn us toward our inner wisdom.
- Jump, and the net will appear. (Robin Crow)
- Inch by inch, life is a cinch. (Mac Anderson)
- If you feel stuck, the best antidote is positive action.
- You'll find comfort in doing something.
- Find someone you can trust to be your guide.
- Resist overwhelming yourself with self-doubt, confusion, or fear.
- The fog of self-doubt makes it difficult to see a problem objectively.
- The Gap is real... it's a universal experience.

Personal Reflections:

1. Think of a transition as the wilderness.
   - What would you do—or not do—if you were lost?
   - How can those solutions be applied to a life transition?

2. Making decisions too slowly or too quickly when you're stuck in life can be equally problematic.
   - Do you tend to make decisions too slowly or too quickly?
   - What are the consequences of the speed with which you make decisions?
   - What are the more likely consequences if you were to speed up or slow down?

3. If you are feeling immobilized, write one, two, or three simple, specific steps you can take to move forward—inch by inch.

4. If you are in transition or anticipating a difficult transition, is there someone whom you trust, who is balanced in his or her thinking, who will tell you the truth, and who will listen and not judge who can be your guide?

Chapter 6

Your Mind's Culture

We've all heard the phrase, "Perception is reality." Consider the strongly held beliefs that lay on opposing sides of political systems, religions, and even competitive sports, and how so many people can't be persuaded past their stands on that slippery thing called reality. This is the power of perception. There's some *reality* involved in every perception, but what we call reality lies largely in the eye of the beholder.

When you face a major transition, think about how busy your mind is, trying to make sense of what's going on while attempting to predict what might happen next; and worse, you can't get your mind off how things used to be. Indeed, much is going on inside your head each waking hour; it's nearly unstoppable, and the level of activity goes up wildly in times of change. There was a lot going on in my mind when I found myself stuck in the Gap, and that's what made the experience so intense and confusing. I'm sure you can relate.

However, the reality is that managing your mind (that is, monitoring your attitude, perceptions, expectations, and otherwise thoughts) is easier said than done. But the *good* news is that you can control much of what goes on in your head if you're willing to work at it. By monitoring your thoughts and keeping yourself more rational, you can prevent a situation from spinning out of control. Your current way of thinking, perceiving, and responding to events is a habit you've developed over time, and any learned habit can be unlearned, improved, or changed if we're motivated to do so.

Think About How You Think

If you tend to be a worrier, or you regularly carry a hefty load of stress, you will benefit mightily from paying more attention to what goes on in your mind. My suggestion is to practice your mental skills *now*, so they will be there when you need them. As you well know, life is unpredictable, and an unanticipated change could drop in your lap at any moment.

A sudden, big life shift (death, accident, illness, or job loss) can leave us feeling abandoned, lost, and forsaken. But a disciplined and rational mind can sort through and rein in intense emotions more effectively than a disorderly, emotional one. Think of world-class athletes, for example, who perform coolly and effectively under great pressure. They and their coaches would tell you that the secret to successful performance lies more in the mind than the body. As Lance Armstrong famously said, "It's not about the bike."

Note that in discussing the skill of mind management, I'm not suggesting that you can breeze through extreme or profound loss such as the death of a loved one, a traumatic divorce, terminal diagnosis, or any circumstance that involves raw grieving. But in time, even the emotional pain of loss can be eased when a person can separate the rational from the irrational and the possible from the impossible. We all handle grief in our ways, and while I wouldn't presume to tell you how to grieve, I hope the ideas in this chapter could help you through a difficult time when you face a major loss.

Meet Your Mind's Culture

You are probably familiar with the term *corporate culture*. All our social systems from nations to organizations to communities and even families have their culture. This culture, developed over time, is driven by collective beliefs, policies, shared values, and norms, evident by expressed attitudes and behaviors. Call it tradition, heritage, or lifestyle; most people conform to the cultural influences surrounding them. If you've ever heard anyone say, "This is how we do things around here," whether the person was describing a company or family, you were given a lesson about its culture.

Some organizational cultures are conservative and highly structured where rules and procedures are strictly followed (think bureaucracy). In this environment, those who operate outside cultural norms are reined in, punished, or encouraged to leave. Task-focused cultures are more concerned about getting results; they're more of a "did you do it" and less "how did you do it" atmosphere. It's always helpful to identify cultural norms before you take a new job to ensure you're in the right place for your style.

Cultures sometimes change. CEOs who find their corporations falling behind the times might start a culture shift to stay viable in a changing marketplace. They might change their image, internal policies, management style, brand, and even the physical environment to show the transformation. So what's my point? In any social system, if you want to change people's behavior, you first must change their attitudes.

With all that said, you have a mental culture similar to the human or social systems described above. Your surroundings shape and influence your *mind's culture*. In other words, your reality is the result of your perceptions and mental filters, which compose the core of your mind's culture. You can trace your behavior, and often the results you get in life, back to your thoughts, beliefs, and norms in your mind's culture. It works like this: what or how you *see* things affects how you behave, what you *do*. In other words, if you *envision* failure, you *do* nothing, therefore *get* nothing.

The Core of Mind Management: PEPA

To make it easier to understand *mind management*, I've developed a model and acronym I call "PEPA." First, you should know that it represents the four ways in which your mind's culture manifest's itself, and they are your:

- Perceptions
- Expectations
- Problem/Solution Orientation
- Attitude

Further, however, understanding this model offers you a way to practice mind management. Another way to look at this model is to suggest that the four components are the *manifestations* of your mind's culture; that is, how you perceive, your expectations, whether you are stuck on problems or seek solutions, and your attitude are all outcomes of how you think.

Your attitude, how you view the world and respond to it, is the result of your experience. Unfortunately, human nature being what it is, negative experiences might have had the greatest influence on the development of your mind's culture; research shows that negative emotions tend to affect us in a greater way than positive emotions do. When asked to think of a happy moment from the past, people often have difficulty recalling one, but when asked about a sad or very negative event, it readily comes to mind, suggesting that negative emotions and events tend to be more intense and longer remembered.

The residue of childhood traumas and other unfortunate incidents tend to make us cautious, guarded, or filled with self-doubt. These influences often hold us back or plague us when we feel confused, pressured, or vulnerable.

You can trace your behavior and results back to your thoughts and beliefs.

Imagine for a moment that, while growing up, you were told repeatedly that you were dumb as a stump and always made stupid decisions. This negative influence could easily become embedded in your mind's culture and dictate the way you behave as an adult. Any such traumatic history can undermine self-confidence or foster indecisiveness. Knowing that culture influences attitude, think about how difficult it would be to manage a successful transition with this attitude.

Our mind's culture drives our thoughts—and vice versa. Our thoughts drive our behavior. Our behavior results in consequences or outcomes that support whatever exists in our inner culture. If you're thinking this all sounds like the chicken or egg puzzle, you're on the right track. But the good news is that the mind's culture is dynamic.

It can slowly evolve or suddenly change, depending on the circumstances and depending on you.

Let's take an in-depth look at the mind management components and how these core competencies can help you better manage your mind. To manage your mind's culture you must:

- Clarify Your **P**erceptions
- Manage Your **E**xpectations
- Realize **P**roblems, but Focus on Solutions
- Choose Your **A**ttitude

Clarify Your Perceptions

Perceptions are the foundation of our behavior. I literally can't take a step without first perceiving that the ground I'm standing on will support me. However, I've had enough experience to be confident in this perception; I don't think about the steps I take unless my circumstances change to require walking more carefully. For instance, if I'm crossing an icy patch or working on the roof, I know I need to pay attention. As such, my increased awareness alters my perception, causing me to move more carefully.

Whether we are walking, driving our cars, or operating power tools, our perception of physical reality is largely based on evidence and experience. But it's a different story with *emotional* or *subjective* perceptions; our unconsciously ingrained, unquestioned, or unexplored perceptions have a great impact on our mind's culture, which in turn affects our behavior and the outcomes we create.

As Thoreau said, we don't see the world as it is, but as we are. Perception is personal, subjective, and highly variable. Think about all existing social biases and that they are largely perceptual and not reality-based. Rather than thinking of perceptions as good or bad, we need to regard them as subject to exploration and evaluation **so we**

don't operate under false premises. It is only through questioning, testing, and *clarifying* our perceptions that we can correctly distinguish between objective reality and our invention of it.

During significant transitions, where we face unfamiliar territory and feel so alone, our minds can play tricks on us. It is crucial and essential to question, test, and challenge our perceptions constantly during these difficult periods. For example, spouses who endure abusive marriages might perceive that they are stuck where they are with no possible way out. Those who end a long-term unhappy marriage might perceive that life will be filled with bliss once the divorce is final. Are both of these interpretations accurate or subjective? You get the point. Go for clarity; constantly challenge your perceptions; don't let yourself be caught up in distorted versions of what you call reality. You'll thank yourself later for doing the work.

Manage Your Expectations

In my less mature days, I had a frustration meter that always seemed maxed out. Thanks to my desire to learn and grow emotionally—and my wife and soul mate Jane who had the courage to keep me in check—I learned to manage my expectations. It's easy to forget that expectations are a huge part of our mind's culture because expectations continually influence our thoughts and perceptions. Expectations are subtle, and we often don't realize their presence until we experience disappointment or disillusionment. They lurk undetected in the background of our minds, yet they drive choices we make about how and where we live, what kinds of careers we choose, and even the selection of our mates. The fallout from our unrecognized, unrealistic, and unmet expectations can be gigantic.

I urge you to explore your assumptions and expectations so you can be more aware of their influence. Here's a slightly pedestrian but very common example. When I check out of a hotel, employees usually ask, "Was everything OK?" If I say, "Not really," I see facial expressions telling me that they fully expected a yes.

Occasionally, when I'm paying for an excellent dining or lodging experience, I might ask for the manager. The person waiting on me might flash one of those "deer in the headlights" expressions followed by a pause, and then a tentative "Is there anything I can help you with?" I reply, "No, I just wanted to pass along my appreciation for the great service here." I love the look of surprise and relief that follows, because most of the time, when people ask for the manager, it's to complain, not to compliment. Over time, employees develop a set of expectations about customers asking to "talk to the boss." This is their mind's culture in action. And to the earlier point about perceptions, if you follow this story to the end and if the employee didn't ask, "Is there anything I can help you with?" and just set off to find the manager, what do you think would be the result for that employee? Stress! At least until they later learned why I wanted to see the manager.

So that you don't operate under false premises, subject your perceptions to evaluation and exploration.

The employee's asking for clarification was the right thing to do.

In my work as a personal development coach, I often help people or groups in conflict. As such, I can attest that unmet expectations are often at the root of a dispute. Whenever we feel disappointed, let down, or angry about something, it's because our expectations weren't met. We spend most of our waking hours in expectation mode, and in nearly every effort or interaction, we have some expectation how things will or should be.

Perhaps one of my bigger lessons as a father was in teaching and grooming my daughters to be good tennis players. I recall with my oldest that in seeing early that she had great potential, I unintentionally created in her the expectation that, given her natural talent, she would always win her matches. As her coach and cheerleader, I lavished her with positive reinforcement about how talented she was. But at age 8, when she lost her first real match, I didn't expect that she would start bawling at the top of her lungs. My constant praise about her talent created the expectation in her that she would automatically win. Only then did I realize it would have served her better had I emphasized hard work, patience, and the enjoyment of the game. This was a lesson for me as a parent about the need to help my children manage their expectations. I indeed applied this lesson with my second daughter. Now as teenagers, I think they will both tell you that although I still encourage them and offer positive reinforcement, I emphasize, "Hard work and commitment are the keys to success."

If you want to master the skill of mind management, you must manage your expectations, which takes much self-awareness and considerable work because expectations are seldom at the forefront of our minds. Having to identify your unmet expectations and feel the rush of accompanying dismay or disillusionment is often the first obstacle in a transition.

Being able to manage your expectations will help you handle the everyday stress and conflict that can arise at any time, but it's an essential skill when you're in the throes of a transition where emotional sensitivity can be so intense. I'm sure you're aware that moving toward an unknown destination can conjure all kinds of expectations, so the more self-aware you are, the more effective you'll be in maintaining a realistic, well-grounded attitude.

Realize Problems/Focus on Solutions and Your Perimeter of Personal Power

When I was in the Air Force and stationed at a small base in New Mexico, the base held war games, realistic training exercises that simulate battle. My role was to be part of the enemy team whose job it was to infiltrate various secure compounds and other guarded areas on the base. One maneuver involved attempting to penetrate a field perimeter set up by security forces that protected a tented command post, the "brains" of any armed force.

We often attempted to invade under the cover of darkness while the security forces remained secured in bunkers, waiting for us to show our faces. They watched in silence, trying to remain alert as they surveyed the dark, unsure of what, if anything, would happen, or when. As the attackers, we knew we could inflict some mental distress by doing nothing. The waiting forces were left to wonder what we might be thinking and doing and when we might attack.

After one such exercise, I asked some security force professionals how they dealt with the uncertainty. It seemed that in a real wartime situation, a perimeter guard could go nuts, having to sit so still for so long while trying to figure what the enemy was up to. I wondered if this gave the enemy a psychological advantage over the guarding force. Without blinking an eye, the sergeant retorted with a surprising answer, "You're not a problem for me until you attempt to break through our perimeter, and *then*, it would become *your* problem, wouldn't it?"

I got it. I realized that this man knew where his real power lay, inside the perimeter. He understood the problem was out there, but he more understood that he could only control what was approaching or within the marked perimeter, and that was it. What lay outside the perimeter was beyond his scope. The sergeant (and his team) weren't going to attempt to control anything or anyone until it was within his *sphere of control*.

We can generalize this example into the context of life and its inevitable transitions. At one time in my life, I made few distinctions between my sphere of control and what lay beyond it. In other words, I could spend inordinate time worrying about things I could do nothing about. As a child, I remember worrying about what would happen if my parents died or if the Russians were going to direct a nuclear missile our way.

I haven't mastered this to the degree I'd like, and thus random worries still pop into my head from time to time. But I've learned not to waste my precious, limited time or energy on things I can do nothing about. I recognize that there are many uncontrollable and unpredictable forces in life, and it's my job to accept this reality. I might be unable to change or control much of what goes on around me, but I can anticipate and prepare myself to some extent, so I'm at least partly ready to handle what crosses into my perimeter.

As you know, it's helpful to recognize when you are needlessly wringing your hands and lamenting about things you can't control. However, you're much better off saving your energy and power for when you need to be positive, productive, or pro-active. I encourage you to focus your energy and creativity on the things

Focus on your Perimeter of Personal Power: Don't waste energy on things you can do nothing about.

you can change and affect, the issues and matters that exist inside your perimeter. That's your center, your sphere of control. And that's where your power lies.

In this regard, the key in transition is not to be stuck on the problem. Recognize the problem, but focus on finding solutions as soon as possible. For instance, if some negative event such as divorce caused the change and transition, you must look back to help you understand where things went wrong and so forth. Too often, folks stay focused on the problem—they stay angry, frustrated, in blaming mode, in grief, thinking about revenge and all the things that keep your mind in the past. Rather, I encourage you at the earliest point possible to decide that its time to move on and seek solutions. The sooner you begin to practice this aspect of mind management, the more productive your transition will be and the sooner you will reach your new world.

Choose Your Attitude

If you've read any biographies of famous people who've gone through a serious struggle in life, you know that some people deal with adversity better than others do. The ability to face and handle challenging situations is often called mental toughness. Knowing that athletes are taught how to keep cool under pressure tells us that resilience might be less a case of temperament and more a case of consciously developed habits. Compare the negative attitude of "Things never work out for me!" with the positive "I'll give it my best shot," and you can predict the likely outcomes of each perspective. The dominant thought patterns existing in our mind's culture are subtle and habitual, and we need to learn if we are unconsciously programming ourselves to fail or succeed.

When our daughter Christina, at the ripe old age of 4, got into trouble for misbehaving, we watched her wail and moan in despair, exclaiming, "This is the worst day of my life!" Chuckling to myself at her drama queen moment, I could only wonder what her DQ quotient might be in another 10 years. From there, I wondered if I should put myself in therapy now, so by the time she and Alexandra (her younger sister) were teens, I could handle all the drama and trauma through which they might put me.

Joking aside, mind management works. Although I haven't mastered my attitude, I've come a long, long way. However, I am clear about the enormous influence a healthful attitude plays in everyday life, and even more, the significant role it plays in handling change and transition. Attitude has everything to do with how you behave, and it is intimately connected to the results you get in life. Whatever your outlook, positive or negative, your attitude creates its self-reinforcing system. Henry Ford once said, "Whether you think you can or you think you can't, you're right." Your mind is a powerhouse without limits, capable of taking you to new depths—or heights.

Perhaps the most compelling thing I have learned about attitude is that *it is a choice*. In the mid-1990s, I became associated with the Covey Leadership Center, and thus began to study the works of Dr. Stephen R. Covey. Through this study, I was introduced to the insights of Dr. Viktor Frankl, an Austrian psychologist who wrote about his experiences and observations during his captivity in several Nazi concentration camps. Among his many profound thoughts was his notion that "everything can be taken from a man [or woman] but one thing—the last of the human freedoms —to choose one's attitude in any given set of circumstances." During every moment of every day, each of us is only a decision away from choosing—good over bad, love over hatred, giving over keeping, and growing over stagnating. This is good news.

The bad news is that "choosing your attitude" falls into the camp of "easy to understand, difficult to build into a consistent way of life." Yet, it's not an all-or-none proposition. An instant and complete shift from a negative to a positive attitude might not be possible. However, you can learn, grow, and improve. Start with self-awareness, taking notice of your current, typical attitude toward the world around you. Pay attention to what you think and how you react to things. If it's always negative and unproductive, learn to shift in the moment— recognize that your attitude is a choice and decide to have a different one. Once you begin to feel and see the power of choosing your attitude, you will continue to change.

Your attitude entering into and within a transition is crucial. It determines the steps you take and the results you get. You can step into a transition and choose your attitude, to which you will then see a crisis or opportunity, you're sinking or swimming, you are traversing stepping-stones or obstacles, or that you are a victim or someone who fights back. Your attitude could ultimately lead you to be someone destined to succeed or destined to fail. The practice of mind-management is a journey and process. Work hard at it, and you will develop a healthier mindset fit for all occasions.

Summary of "Your Mind's Culture" (How You Think):

- You control much of what goes on in your head.
- Any learned habit can be unlearned, improved, or changed.
- Practice your mental skills now, so they will be there when you need them.
- A disciplined and rational mind can sort through and rein in intense emotions more effectively than a disorderly, emotional one.
- Your surroundings shape and influence your mind's culture.
- You can trace your behavior and results back to your thoughts, beliefs, and norms in your mind's culture.
- Your perceptions, expectations, problem/solution orientation, and attitude are the manifestations of your mind's culture.
- Negative experiences tend to have the greatest influence on your mind's culture.
- Perceptions are the foundation of our behavior.
- We don't see the world as it is, but as we are. (Thoreau)
- Regard perceptions as "subject to exploration and evaluation so we don't operate under false premises." Go for clarity; constantly challenge your perceptions.
- Expectations are subtle, and we often don't realize their presence—explore them so you can be more aware of their influence.
- Focus on your *Perimeter of Personal Power*: Don't waste time or energy on things you can do nothing about. Focus on things you can change and significantly affect.
- Attitude is intimately connected to the results you get in life.
- Pay attention to what you think and how you react to things. If it's always negative and unproductive, learn to shift in the moment.

Personal Reflections:

1. Our perceptions shape our behavior.

   - How might perceptions stand in your way of transitioning smoothly?
   - How can you ensure your perceptions are accurate before acting?

2. How would you describe your general prevailing attitude?

   - Are you usually positive or optimistic?
   - Or do you tend to be negative?
   - How might your attitude influence your outcomes in life?
   - If you could *choose* your attitude about your current transition, what would it be?

3. Is there something about which you're worrying? Is it within your personal power to change it? If not, what would it take to let go of the problem or the worrying?

Chapter 7

The Best Laid Plans

According to John Lennon, "Life is what happens while you're making other plans." If you're expecting a significant change or are in the midst of one, you need to manage your expectations before you can effectively manage the situation. Try to be as realistic as possible about current conditions and eventual outcomes so you don't end up surprise and stunned. Life is unpredictable, and even the most organized plans can take unexpected twists. The most effective approach is to anticipate disruptions and changes in directions or approach. There might be times when you are forced to regroup because your expectations were out of sync with that thing we call reality.

Derailed: Expectations Gone Awry

I touched on expectations in chapter 6. However, I believe that dealing with expectations is so relevant and important to transition that we should delve deeper into it.

When I began to transition from the Air Force, I worked off a plan I'd been formulating for more than 3 years. During my years of military service, I knew I would make my exit at the 20-year mark, which gave me a lot of time to think about my transition and make some plans.

However, even with what I thought was a solid plan in place, things did not go as expected, at least not for the first few years. Being swiftly derailed stopped me in my tracks. I thought I had designed a great plan where more or less everything would work out as I had envisioned, but as things began to unfold in a different direction, my frustration morphed into concern and then panic; that's when I knew I was in trouble.

When I planned and visualized my transition, the expectation was that I would shift smoothly from the structure and discipline of military culture into civilian life and a new career. For instance, in the military, there is an underlying culture and expectation that you plan and things are done. Further, there is a collaborative culture that you can rely on others to do their part and on time. Don't get me wrong, things go off course and schedule, but the general culture is such that one gets used to the structure and discipline of staying on course and on top of the mission at hand. Thus, getting off course and somewhat losing control flew in the face of my assumptions and expectations and left me perplexed. I began a tailspin.

In retrospect, I did not attend well enough to the element of "expecting the unexpected." When you approach or are in a major life transition where you are entering a place of significant unknowns, expecting the unexpected is a much bigger dragon to slay. If I had attended to this idea more, I'm certain I could have handled my crisis differently. Now, consider that I understood the idea of managing expectations, and I had put together a good plan, I thought I was covered for about anything, but I wasn't. So I want to encourage you to think this through and then think again. It's that important.

Expecting The Unexpected

It is often said that hindsight is always 20/20, and I agree. There's nothing like the passing of time to give us perspective. As I look back on what I learned and how I grew from being stuck in the Gap, only now do I realize that things did unfold as they should—meaning I learned from being stuck and perhaps it was what I needed to learn. Part of what I learned was that my first expectations didn't include the aspects of my life that were beyond my control, such as how much time it would take for my plan to get traction, how others would respond to my ideas, and many large and small unnamed stumbling blocks I would encounter. With the best of plans, again, when you are venturing into uncharted territory, *adaptation* and *managing expectation* **must** be key words in your self-talk vocabulary. I now know that managing expectations involves more than creating a plan.

At some point in your life, you have probably been told to "expect the worst, but hope for the best," and if you don't take it too literally, there is much wisdom in that adage. I'm not suggesting that you be a pessimist, but part of managing your expectations is acknowledging up front that you are not in control of everything and that, by their very nature, transitions bring with them many unknown elements. The unknowns, the unpredictable and uncontrollable factors, make it impossible to have an ironclad plan that will neatly unfold as you hoped. Even when you "expect the unexpected," there will still be surprises. The more open you are to this reality, the more you will be able to tolerate, accept, and handle the unplanned factors and derailments that come your way.

The foundation for managing expectations is first to acknowledge that there are indeed many unknowns. Circumstances can, and will, change. You need a plan, and I recommend you write it all out (many studies suggest that "putting it in writing" increases the likelihood of achieving your goals). So let's put it this way—it can't hurt you, unless you expect that your plans are carved in stone. Maintain an open mind and be willing to adapt as unexpected events arise.

Another essential ingredient in managing expectations has to do with remaining rational or objective about the uncontrollable factors existing around you. For example, I once had little patience for traffic jams, and the morning and evening rush hours frustrated me to no end. I grumbled to anyone who would listen about how irritating it was, being stuck on congested roads twice a day. My wife got the

> *Putting your goals in writing increases the likelihood of achieving them.*

brunt of my frustrations. Finally, Jane began to remind me (actually, scold me) before I left the house, preparing me for the inevitable.

She would say, "Kevin, you know there will be heavy traffic out there, so accept it *now*, before you get in the car. Say to yourself, there *will* be traffic jams, so be prepared for them. Accept that there will be all kinds of cars on the road. This isn't something you can control, and the stress will eventually kill you if you don't get over it!" Was I so irrational back then that I thought perhaps my frustration could make the cars disappear, and I'd have the road to myself? It's that perception and reality thing again: I was nearly making myself sick over an uncontrollable circumstance, not once, but twice a day. This is a perfect example of how expectations get in the way of acceptance.

My wife's not so subtle reminders helped me manage my mind and my expectations about the inescapable traffic and the unnecessary stress I was inflicting on myself. I had to come to terms with the fact that, however frustrated I became, my feelings would not unclog the traffic or make bad drivers disappear. I had to use this process to get unstuck and free myself from the Gap.

Start to pay more attention to your expectations. At first, you might not even realize you have particular expectations until after the fact. By this, I mean, whenever you feel disappointed, confused, angry, or depressed, trace the feeling backward, and you'll become clearer on what expectations you had about the situation. Perhaps you assumed your spouse would be more empathetic or that a friend would stand by you after a crisis. I suggest that you take a letdown from the past and analyze it, using this process of following the path from your feelings to the triggering event. By taking the time to sort your underlying assumptions about people or significant events in your life, you'll be better prepared for future transitions or challenges. You'll be less likely to be derailed by your unmet expectations.

Damage Control: Reminders for Regrouping

If you have ever had to stop, re-evaluate your situation, and clean up the fallout from unrealistic or mismanaged expectations, you might remember the sinking sensation of having to regroup and start the process all over again. "Frustrating" barely describes what it feels like, but you have to settle down and regain your bearings before you can readjust your expectations and make your next move.

Perhaps you remember when you learned how to drive, and you were taught to stay in your lane. You probably assumed or expected that every other driver would do the same, and everything would be fine. But there have been moments when you've unknowingly drifted into another lane, or a driver has done the same to you. You quickly realize you are in danger and act instantly, swerving away from the oncoming vehicle and perhaps even running off the edge of road to prevent a collision. In a few minutes, your pumping heart settles down, you regroup, and you are on your way again, only this time, you are much more aware of the cars around you. The experience parallels what happens when mismanaged expectations run your transition off the road. With any luck, once the narrow escape is over, you brush yourself off, hike up your self-awareness, and get back on the road, headed toward your destination.

Just as with steering a car, your transition might come close to a calamity, unless you stop or change your course. Your first step is to do a self-check, so you can figure out what's gone wrong. Sit down, breathe, and relax as much as you can to clear your head. Ask yourself some searching questions to help you stay as objective as possible:

- *Am I truly off track?*
- *If so, how far off am I, and how serious is this?*
- *What were my expectations?*
- *What underlying assumptions must I let go of?*
- *How can I stabilize myself?*
- *What are my new expectations, and are they based in reality?*
- *What do I need to do next so I can regroup?*

Once you help yourself regroup, you might realize that things are not as bad as they first seemed. Avoid self-criticism; you are not dumb, stupid, or unbalanced. Remember that you are vulnerable now, that you can completely control very few factors, and feelings or moments of self-doubt are normal and temporary. If you discover that your first plan was flawed, make the necessary adjustments, and take the next step. If you need support, reach out for it, whether a friend, counselor, spouse, or your spiritual advisor. Take your time, and do what you need so you can move on. Concisely, damage control and regrouping help you regain (or maintain) a semblance of balance so you can manage the present while keeping an eye on the future.

Mind over Matter

Again, in a previous chapter, I discussed the factors accounting for athletic success and that wise coaches prefer a combination of enough talent and extraordinary determination to exceptional talent and an uninspired attitude. Although success in any endeavor requires talent and skill, the crucial component of ultimate success lies in the mind. Some exceptionally talented and intelligent people will operate at a mediocre level their entire lives, and they have no idea

Don't allow your self-limiting beliefs to keep you from exploring the possibilities.

what's holding them back. Perhaps you know some people who are brilliant, but they could never get their act together because of their limiting beliefs.

In any endeavor, from athletic pursuits to surviving a trauma, success or failure often comes down to mind over matter. Surely, the lack of skill or ability can impede success, but big things happen when you decide to take a class, read a book, or work at developing the skills you need. It helps to know that acquiring new knowledge, skills, and abilities can be frustrating. Learning, by its very nature, involves trying, failing, regrouping, and eventual mastery, if we persist. Pity the faint-hearted who stall when the going gets tough, who allow their limiting beliefs to keep them at least from exploring the possibilities.

Limiting beliefs are the unquestioned and often mistaken assumptions we hold about our abilities. Your belief system is the bedrock of your mind's culture, influencing your perceptions, attitude, and expectations. To be successful in any endeavor, including complex, challenging transitions, you will need to become aware of your assumptions and limiting beliefs so you can counter or mitigate their negative effects.

Tony Robbins speaks about limiting beliefs in his programs. He suggests that the primary reason we don't experience financial success is that we have negative associations with having more money than we need. Our first instinct might be to doubt or dismiss this notion because most of us are unaware of our limiting beliefs and that they hold us back. Our counterarguments are often disguised as justification or rationalization, which keeps us from breaking free of our biases. The author Richard Bach once said, "Argue for your limitations, and sure enough, they're yours." Ironic isn't it that sometimes we doggedly fight to hold ourselves back.

Head First

I recall growing up and believing that I would not go to college because college was for rich or intelligent people. I held that conviction and protected my belief by repeating it. It held me back. Truth be told, I held myself back. And I didn't even realize it. Many of our limiting beliefs are established in childhood when we are too young to question or challenge them. Unless we consciously confront our early assumptions and beliefs, we ease into adulthood, accepting our notions as true.

Sir Roger Bannister's story is a classic example of limiting beliefs. In the sport of track and field, it was accepted that a human being could not run a mile in less than 4 minutes. In his attempt to distinguish himself as a world-class runner, Bannister, a British medical student, decided to break the 4-minute mile. On May 6, 1954, Roger Bannister broke the record with a time of 3:59.4. Until then, athletes, sportswriters, and even the medical community, had shared the limiting belief that it was impossible for a human being to run a mile in less than 4 minutes. Only 46 days later, the Australian runner John Landy broke Bannister's time by a full second. Since that time, dozens of athletes, including some high school students, have gone on to break the 4-minute mile. In case you wonder, the closest a woman has come to breaking the record is 4:12.56, and who knows, it could happen in our lifetime.

Bannister's breakthrough stands as inspiration for us all to examine common assumptions masked as truth, so we can move beyond the beliefs that limit our scope and keep us from achieving our potential.

Breaking Through Barriers

Napoleon Hill, author of the bestselling book, *Think and Grow Rich*, said, "Man, alone, has the power to transform his thoughts into physical reality; man, alone, can dream and make his dreams come true." He also coined the phrase, "What the mind of man can conceive and believe, it can achieve."

Hill was convinced that all great achievers understand the power of thought, and when people convert that thought into a belief and act on it, they can break through barriers. Hill also posited that limiting thoughts or beliefs could stop us from even trying. Believe that you can be successful, and let yourself be surprised at the outcomes. I encourage you to ask yourself how you might be limiting your abilities or choices, based on the beliefs you hold. Here are some ways to identify and overcome limiting belief.

Small Steps, Big Difference

1. **Recognize.** First, teach yourself to distinguish between limiting beliefs and external obstacles. The real obstacles are obvious. If you stand next to a 10-foot fence, you know from experience that you can't jump over it. Unless you were born with springs on

the soles of your feet, jumping that high is a physical impossibility. This is pure physics: it's observable and measurable. On the other hand, limiting beliefs can be as daunting as a 10-foot fence, but they aren't real. They are constructs we erect in our minds. Whenever you are stopped or you feel derailed, ask yourself if you are facing a true and real barrier or a limiting belief. Even huge obstacles can be dealt with. Perhaps you've already figured out that the external hurdles lying in your path are usually easier to clear than the obstructions existing in your head.

2. **Review.** Because limiting beliefs can be such looming barriers, clearly you must *believe* in your ability to achieve your goal. Internalize the idea that you already have what you need to be successful. Review the lessons you've learned in life, consider all you've achieved despite adversities, and reflect on the skills you have mastered so far in this adventure called life. Let the sum of what you've achieved stand as proof of your abilities. Don't be falsely modest. Avoid focusing on your mistakes or failures, and instead, home in on the lessons you have learned. Accept that much of our wisdom comes from the "I'll never do that again" experiences. Let your achievements speak for themselves; don't argue with them, and let your sum of experiences be a continuing source of encouragement.

3. **Reframe.** Pay attention to your self-talk. These are the self-judging, self-defeating thoughts that consistently run through your head. The statements that foster limiting beliefs are often planted in childhood, and as we grow up, we unconsciously cultivate them. Listen carefully to what goes on in your head so you can identify your limiting self-talk patterns and reframe them into affirming statements instead. Some of these early

messages might have been accurate at one time in the past, in one situation, or in one instance, but by internalizing the message, we allow it to generalize into who we always are. Examples might be "My family was right. I'm a lousy decision maker," or "I hate cold calling. There's no way I can make a living doing this."

Once you have a clear idea of a limiting thought running through your head (believe me, there are all kinds), you are ready to reframe that incorrect assumption. Write (yes, don't just think it) a positive statement that refutes your old limiting belief. Avoid negatives such as "I won't." Express your reframed statement in present tense, as if you have already achieved it, and repeat it

Your thoughts can hold you back, or propel you forward.

as many times a day as you can. For instance, "I am an effective decision maker," and "Cold calling gives me an opportunity to meet with new customers who need my products or services."

Some people dismiss the power of self-talk, but let me state, without qualification, that reframing your negative statements is one of the most empowering, potentially life-altering decisions you can make. Research is continually being done on the power of thought, and here's what we need to know—*our brains accept our consistent, persistent thoughts as reality.*

Hard work and positive self-talk are the secrets to record-breaking athletic achievement, business success, or dismal failure. You have a powerhouse of a computer in your head, and it's your job to program it properly, so you can achieve your goals, fulfill your dreams, and make your difficult transitions less traumatic. As Henry Ford said, "If you think you can, or cannot, you're right." Yes, it's that simple.

Imagine facing a huge change, loss, or major shift in your life and being able to sort rationally through your fears, doubts, and limiting beliefs instead of being victimized by them. Envision being able to keep your feet on the ground as you work your way through the repercussions of a big transition. I'm not suggesting that these three steps will guarantee that life's road will always be free of detours, but I can assure you that the route will be much less jarring once you internalize these essential skills. Practice and constant repetition are the keys to reprogramming that amazing mainframe, your brain, so you can better navigate the changes life has in store for you. I urge you to remember always that your thoughts can hold you back or propel you.

Summary of "Best Laid Plans":

- Life is unpredictable, and even the most organized plans can take unexpected twists.
- When venturing into uncharted territory, *adaptation* and *managing expectation* **must** be key words in your vocabulary.
- You are not in control of everything.
- Putting your goals in writing increases the likelihood of achieving them.
- Sometimes you must settle down, regain your bearings, before you can make your next move.
- Pity those who allow their limiting beliefs to keep them from exploring the possibilities.
- To be successful in transitions, you need to become aware of your assumptions and limiting beliefs so you can counter their negative effects.
- It is ironic that, sometimes, we doggedly fight to hold ourselves back.
- What the mind of man or woman can conceive and believe, they can achieve. (Napoleon Hill)
- Listen to what goes on in your head so you can identify your limiting self-talk patterns.
- If you think you can, or cannot, you're right. (Henry Ford).
- Your thoughts can hold you back or propel you forward.

Personal Reflections:

1. Are you currently in a transition you think has gone off track? Ask yourself the following questions:

   - Am I truly off track? If so, what is the evidence—why do you think you're off track?
   - How far off am I?
   - What were my expectations—where should I be?
   - What underlying assumptions must I let go of?
   - How can I stabilize myself?
   - What are my new expectations, and are they based in reality?
   - What do I need to do to get back on track or regroup?

2. If you are in a transition or see one in your future, write down and distinguish between what you know are facts about the transition and what your assumptions are.

3. You are more likely to be successful if you have goals.

   - If you're in The Gap, do you have goals formulated to help you through?
   - Are they written down?
   - Do you review them regularly?
   - Do you adapt them as you transition or change?

4. What might you be doing (perhaps unconsciously) that is holding you back?

Chapter 8

Facing Adversity

I ask not for a lighter burden, but for broader shoulders.

— Jewish Proverb

In some ways, life is a continuing adventure in adversity. The shock of being born, our continual clash with gravity as we stand upright, and the pain of loss are all examples of adversity, from minor challenges to major calamities. Any significant life shift or transition will surely bring with it some level of adversity. You can count on that, and you've probably figured out that making your way through the Gap successfully is all about how you handle adversity.

As circumstances, changes, or shifts in our lives create some level of hardship or upheaval in our routine, it must be said that adversity, like beauty, lies in the eyes of the beholder. Some transitions, such as moving to a new home across town, are merely inconvenient, whereas others, such as a grim medical diagnosis or loss of a loved one, are very painful and overwhelming. If you have a friend suffering an inconvenient transition, I encourage you to be as accepting as you can. Remembering that change is relative and based on perception, even a small disruption of routine can feel like a significant transitional challenge for some people. When school districts reorganize and teachers are forced to change buildings, some are traumatized by leaving their familiar surroundings. It might be tempting to mock what seems a rigid attitude, but I encourage you to be empathetic instead. You can't force understanding on other human beings. They must accept it on their own.

As one who has been through a few intense spin cycles in my life, I've come to understand what lies beyond hardship and struggle, which has made it less difficult for me to accept life's hard times. None of us would wish for adversity in our lives, but with vision and resourcefulness (and perhaps a little luck), we can gain great personal and spiritual growth when we face our circumstances and emerge from our toughest times.

In an earlier chapter, I stated that we learn more lessons from our bad times than good. It might seem paradoxical, but failure, hardship, and adversity are effective teachers. Yet, as the parent of two daughters and a son, I have always been torn between hoping to protect them from pain and wanting to see them spread their wings and achieve independence.

My wife and I are often tempted to intervene so we can help mitigate our children's pain or suffering. This is one of those difficult areas in parenting. No manuals can tell us when to help or when to back off, and we all try to do our best for each circumstance. We both understand that working through difficulty and challenge is how our children learn and grow.

Preparing for Adversity

As parents, my wife and I realize that we do our children a disservice by trying to save or shield them from harsh experiences because that's where life's richest lessons lie. In her books, author C. Leslie Charles says that opportunity and adversity are constant companions, and I agree. I believe it's a natural law. I believe that the greater the adversity, the greater the potential for growth. You have probably read many stories of those who have faced great adversity yet ended up achieving greatness. Call it trial by fire, going in the eye of the hurricane, or whatever, but the outcome is nothing less than gold. Much good in this world has happened because of struggle, pain, and challenge. From Jesus to Gandhi, from Martin Luther King to Mother Teresa, and even the ever-optimistic Michael J. Fox, the list goes on. We are richer in spirit because of the sacrifices and struggles of these people and more.

The Upheaval of Adversity

I attended an American Veterans Symposium that focused on the goal of developing success strategies to help severely wounded soldiers from the Iraq and Afghanistan Wars transition back to a "normal" life. Many parents, spouses, and friends attended, and they, too, struggled with the injured veterans.

I recall one Marine veteran and his wife who attended the conference. He was the victim of an improvised explosive device, or IED, in Iraq. He had lost much of his physical functionality, including sight, ability to walk well, and some cognitive and communication abilities. Part of the reason for attending the conference was to discuss not only his loss and struggles, but also the great struggles his wife would have and they would have as a couple. Seemingly, they would have a long and very difficult transition from what was once a very normal relationship and family life to one in which he completely relied on her.

Coming from a military family and having seen my father come home after being severely injured in the Vietnam War, somehow, I thought I could relate or understand. But when I listened to them describe the many difficulties they have endured and they would continue to endure, it became apparent that many others and I didn't have a clue.

> *Failure, hardship, and adversity are effective teachers.*

I could feel the pain viscerally as different people spoke about their daily struggles. These were good people, heroically dealing with issues most of us can barely imagine; they have Gaps within Gaps. Their worlds have been turned upside down to the extent that things will never be the same again, not even close. The adversity these soldiers, families, and friends live with is almost inconceivable.

Not all adversity is as regrettable or grim as the above I describe. But despite the physical or emotional form adversity takes, or its level of intensity, it is an inevitable fact of life for you and me. The question is not "Will I encounter adversity?" but "Will I be prepared to deal with adversity?" It's natural not to want to think about adversity or the impact it can have on our lives, but a sequence of adverse events could potentially overwhelm and stop you in your tracks, at least temporarily.

Consider the devastation of a natural calamity such as Hurricane Katrina and the lasting damage that storm wrought—the loss of loved ones, the destruction of homes, physical injury, and financial ruin. This domino effect of adversity, again, creates gaps within gaps. Living with the knowledge that anything can happen to anyone at any moment is difficult, but it's true. Think of the tragic deaths of JFK Jr., his young wife and her sister who died with him, and the great loss their families experienced. Neither fame nor fortune can protect us from the inevitable.

Knowing that life is uncertain and we are all vulnerable to unforeseen incidents can be inspiration for taking time daily to feel grateful for what you have. Your gratitude and realistic perspective can also give you the inner strength to draw from when adversity strikes. This way, you can gain as many lessons and spiritual restoration as possible during times of crisis. Jesus of Nazareth spoke about this a few days before his crucifixion. He said, "Unless a grain of wheat falls into the ground and dies, it will remain a single seed. But if it dies, it will produce many grains of wheat" (John 12:24). Adversity can be a seed to growth and understanding.

Anchors for Weathering the Storm

If you have ever seen a ship, you might have noticed the size of its anchors and that there isn't just one. Even a large vessel is vulnerable to storms. Wind, waves, swells, and surges can toss a ship about unless its anchors are in place to keep it stable. Like ships, we, too, need anchors in our lives to help us maintain our balance and stability in times of hardship or struggle.

Those with no support network in place are intensely vulnerable in times of adversity. The U.S. military understands this and is exceptional at developing and keeping support anchors in place for their personnel and families as they move around the world. Although you might think these global nomads would be vulnerable because of their constant moves from one place to the next, it's just the opposite. Through sponsorship and various support programs, military personnel and their families are informed, often months in advance, about their new location so they have time to prepare themselves for their new environment. They are introduced to their sponsor, and they can take advantage of a vast support system fully available to them during their transition. Yes, they still face challenges, but these military support anchors help answer questions and ease the sense of the unknown.

How about you? Do you have a solid support system in place? What or who are the anchors that will help you through a storm? Because our lives are richer when we have solid connections in our lives and because you never know when you might need them, it's important to keep your support anchors in reach and in good repair always. Here is a checklist to help you determine which of your anchors are in place and which you need to shore up.

1. Friendship Anchor

A good test of friendship is to identify whom you could call in the middle of the night when you have a serious problem or crisis. *To whom could you turn if you needed a shoulder on which to cry?*

2. Financial Anchor

Many people worry that lending or borrowing money is a great way to end a relationship, but it's also a sign of trust and confidence. *Who could or would help you if you suddenly found yourself in financial straits?*

3. Legal Anchor

Not everyone has an attorney on retainer standing by to tackle complex problems that might arise, but there are times in our lives when we need such a resource. *Do you have an attorney, or is there someone you could use if you needed immediate legal counsel?*

4. Community, Social Group, or Church Support Anchor

What community, social group, or church support anchor exists in your life so you can either give or receive help when needed?

5. Advice Anchor

I believe everyone should have a good therapist, counselor, supportive spouse, or wise friend to provide feedback and help you think straight in times of crisis. My wife is my primary advice anchor. I trust her motives, cool head, and common sense approach to life. *Who helps you think straight with his or her wisdom and calming advice?*

6. Challenge Anchor

This one might surprise you. Advice anchors can listen, guide, and suggest, but there are also times when we need someone to cut to the chase and tell us we are off base. The challenge anchor is a logical, direct-speaking friend or counselor who forces us to recognize the error of our ways. *Who challenges your wrongheaded ideas and keeps you in tow when you most need it?*

We need anchors to help us remain stable in the midst of turbulence. The stress of any trauma can obscure your thoughts with fear, doubt, and other emotions to the point that it's hard to think objectively. Your various anchors can help you maintain at least a semblance of stability when your mind is scattered and stressed. From trained counselors or legal professionals to friends, social connections, or spouse, your support anchors can help you find calm in the midst of the storm. You will benefit by keeping each in reach and in good condition.

I encourage you to sit down and identify the support anchors in your life. In the spaces below, or in your journal, if you have one, take a moment to list your anchors by name. If one category remains blank, you know what you need to do. Life is a constant exercise in getting and giving. The more secure and accessible your support anchors are, the easier it will be for you to reach out and ask for help when you need to.

The above exercise might also encourage *you* to consider the list of those for whom you function as a support anchor (and in which category), so you can keep those relationships in good repair and ready. The people we choose and those who choose us as our anchors not only help us keep our feet on the ground, but they also function as a mirror. Anchors let us glimpse, sometimes, our inner wisdom, our hopes and fears, and our behaviors under pressure. These are just a few reasons our anchors are so important.

Reset Your Sails and Regain Your Confidence

Perhaps your spouse or a close friend has commented on how you tend to behave when things fall apart, and if you're open to this feedback, it can help you grow and change for the better. Sometimes, it's helpful to ask yourself how you handle adversity and what your immediate response to a crisis might be. Do you really know? I can guarantee that anyone who spends much time with you could probably make your ears burn if you were to ask them for feedback.

There was a time in my life, when things got difficult, I would get angry with myself for having allowed the situation to happen. Even more, after my anger fit, I'd punish myself with guilt trips—for getting angry or losing control. Neither of these reactions helped my situation, and thank goodness, I figured it out. Thanks to a combination of maturity and self-development, I've changed those reactive tendencies. Now in difficult times, instead of seeing the downside or wasting time being upset

> *Adversity can be a seed to growth and understanding.*

for getting myself into this mess, I search for the deeper meaning behind the circumstance and focus on the potential growth that can come out of it. In other words, I try to find that diamond in the rough.

During times of adversity, your self-confidence and self-esteem will be tested. Take steps to restore it.

As you know, in times of crisis, it's easy to fall into a tailspin where you begin to question your self-worth, abilities, and instincts. You might temporarily lose faith in yourself. Even people with healthy self-esteem can suffer lapses when they find themselves in the Gap. But you can keep your self-regard intact by taking the following precautions:

- Encourage yourself. Remember that self-doubt and a temporary loss of confidence are normal during difficult times.
- Engage in healthful outlets. Immerse yourself in activities you enjoy or are good at, whether it's writing, singing, playing a sport, or any other outlet, even if you have to force yourself to do it.
- Express yourself. Talk with your support anchor, therapist, clergy, or friend. Admit that you're feeling down and lacking your normal level of confidence or self-esteem. Talk it out and listen carefully to words of encouragement.

- Give of yourself. Although it's normal to focus on your problems during difficult times, you might be astounded to discover how much better you'll feel when you reach out to help someone else. Feelings of self-worth and contribution are magnified when you focus on helping others who are in greater need than you are. In getting out of your own little bubble, you might also discover that your situation isn't nearly as awful as you had thought, and there are many people with whom you wouldn't want to change places.

Fighting the Emotional "Drag-ons"

You have a network of core characteristics that fuel your willingness to act and move forward despite a threatening or adverse situation. These inner qualities include your self-esteem, confidence, determination, discipline, motivation, and vision. The level to which you cultivate these essential characteristics is central to your success. You could think of these combined traits as the forces behind your power, not just for change and transition, but also for life in general.

Physics teaches us that, for every action, there is a reaction, and besides your many assets, opposing qualities in you can retard your ability to learn, grow, and change. Consider the opposites of self-esteem, confidence, determination, discipline, motivation, and vision, and you have the forces that feed your limiting beliefs and hold you back. I call them mental drag-ons, emotional baggage that holds you back and drags you down.

In an earlier chapter, I discussed limiting beliefs, and again, I urge you to confront the mistaken notions that keep you from realizing your potential. You especially want to address and overcome these issues before you face a major issue or life shift to make the transition less difficult. Freeing yourself of emotional baggage means you'll travel lighter.

You'll be able to take better advantage of the learning and growth that lies on the other side of the Gap instead of being stuck in a defensive posture where you might end up suffering the same mistakes repeatedly. If you want to make progress in your life, rid yourself of the misguided thoughts and behavior that don't serve you anymore, so they don't haunt or overwhelm you when you face difficult times.

Even if you suffer from early emotional scars, you can minimize their effects on your long-term attitude and behavior. It might take a long time to recover from an early trauma, but you can do it. One example is the prolific author Thich Nhat Hanh, a Buddhist monk exposed to innumerable war atrocities as a child. Today, he writes about peace and acceptance. The adage that obstacles are the stepping-stones to success is a great way to describe human resilience and recovery. Just as with Hanh, a deeper understanding of peace and happiness can come out of experiencing chaos, hardship, and pain. Ask a cancer survivor or anyone else who has had a narrow escape and is all the better for it.

Beyond Emotional Baggage

My close friend once disclosed that when he was about 4, a family adopted him. He said his adoptive father was a violent, physically and verbally abusive man. Not only did my friend suffer extensive abuse as a child, but also those years of adversity contributed to some emotional pain he has struggled with through the years.

Although he now seems to be doing well as an adult, he will tell you that he still carries some pain and feelings of helplessness from growing up in such dire circumstances. During one significant transition, he found himself indecisive and unsure about even small decisions he encountered while in the Gap. Through professional counseling, he discovered that he was stuck in a pattern of second-guessing himself, thanks to the many years of hearing his father tell him how stupid he was and that he couldn't think for himself.

For him, the emotional drag of the weight he carried in his mind immobilized him during times of upheaval and change. "It was like I was being attacked from inside myself. Forget rational decision making; I was so caught up trying to fend off my inner dragon (the fear of making the wrong decision) that I avoided making *any* decisions at all."

Some missing elements in the background of abused children are trust, unconditional support, and acceptance. Fortunately, my friend married an exceptional woman, and they have wonderful children and a wealth of love and affection in their home. He learned to trust, love, and accept being loved, and the richness of his family life helped restore his emotional well-being. My

Good sailors are not made on calm seas.

friend is an example of someone who was not only able to move on despite the emotional drag-ons in his life, but also he gained the insight and understanding that comes from adversity, which helped him leave much of his early pain.

Shedding our emotional burdens allows us to love ourselves, not egotistically, but in a gentle and nonjudgmental way. This sounds like a cliché, but we can freely give love to another only when we truly learn to love and accept ourselves.

When we face adversity, time seems to stand still, and it feels as if this awful period will never go away. Depending on the depth and breadth of our trauma, we might temporarily feel beaten down and broken in spirit. In his book, *The Blessings of Brokenness*, Dr. Charles Stanley suggests that, if we are willing to search for them, blessings ride in on the wake of our being broken, and I agree.

As I see it, God gives us the circumstances that allow us to feel "broken" because, in these moments, if we permit it to happen, God will work with us so we can again feel whole. This doesn't happen overnight; it could take weeks, months, or years to finish the process. Stanley says that this restoration and rebuilding process is a natural part of life and integral to "God's refining and fashioning us."

Dr. Stanley reminds us "that [spiritual] growth is a process that includes setbacks, failures, and hard-won lessons." Whether you are a believer, you might well consider the ideas of resurgence and self-renewal as universal truths. They are the light at the end of the tunnel.

We all know from experience that our feelings of self-doubt, insecurity, and threat are exacerbated during times of upheaval. Those are the times we are most vulnerable to inner demons and external circumstances. Our feelings, perceptions, and expectations become more intense during difficult times. But if you force yourself to think rationally, if you consciously practice positive self-talk to stabilize your emotions, you will empower yourself to make better decisions. Objectivity will enable you to perceive adverse times as opportunities in disguise, allowing you to endure the pain, so you can mend and grow in a way you might not otherwise have conceived.

Beyond Adversity

Knowing that early traumas or painful experiences can retard our emotional development, I encourage you to reflect on your history. What emotional drag-ons exist in your memory bank? I ask this because your painful history can come back to haunt you in times of challenge or transition; it can cloud your judgment and undermine your confidence.

Think about the times in your life when you have felt most vulnerable. Now that you know the power of self-talk, identify the thoughts that overtake you in times of crisis. Reflect on the negative messages you might have heard as a child that caused you to second-guess yourself or feel helpless. If you can't think of any, just pay close attention to your self-talk the next time you screw up. That will give you a clue.

Don't worry; we all have these negative inner voices, and it's mostly an issue of degree. A few grumbles are nothing compared to self-condemnation. And here's the hopeful part—if you find you have a few extra pounds of emotional baggage waiting to trip you up when you most need your strength, confidence, and self-esteem, now is the time to identify them, disarm them, and dump them. You have everything to gain and nothing to lose.

Summary of "Facing Adversity":

- Traversing the Gap *successfully* comes down to how you handle adversity.
- Adversity lies in the eyes of the beholder.
- You can't force understanding on human beings—you must discover and accept it.
- We can gain great personal and spiritual growth when we face our circumstances and emerge from our toughest times.
- Failure, hardship, and adversity are effective teachers.
- Opportunity and Adversity are constant companions. (C. Leslie Charles)
- Take time to be grateful for what you have.
- Adversity can be a seed to growth and understanding.
- Like ships, we, too, need anchors in our lives to help us maintain our balance and stability in times of hardship or struggle.
- Those with no support network in place are intensely vulnerable in times of adversity.
- During times of adversity, your self-confidence and self-esteem will be tested. Take steps to restore it.
- Give of yourself.
- Shedding our emotional burdens allows us to love ourselves.
- Be aware that during times of upheaval our inner "demons" and "drag-ons" rear their ugly heads.
- Practice positive self-talk to stabilize your emotions.

Personal Reflections:

1. Reflect on a time or times in your life when you experienced failure, hardship, or adversity.
   - What negative outcomes resulted from those times?
   - What positive outcomes resulted from those times?
   - What lessons did you learn from those times?
   - How did those times shape the person you are today?

2. Develop the habit of being grateful, which will contribute to a more positive outlook and attitude.
   - Do you take time daily or weekly to reflect on your blessings and give thanks?
   - Do you take the time to thank people for what they do for or say to you?
   - Do you tend to think of the glass as half-full, as opposed to half-empty? If half-empty, what can you do to develop a more optimistic mindset?

3. Do you have a support network in place?
   - Are there people whom you trust to whom you can turn for support in times of need?
   - If not, what steps can you take to create such relationships?

4. Are you carrying emotional burdens that keep you from being the best you can be?
   - What emotional burdens are you carrying?
   - How do they affect your decisions and outlook?
   - How can you unload those burdens so they no longer weigh you down?

Chapter 9

Harnessing Your Personal Power

As a boy, I had an enormous imagination, and like many children, I often pretended to be a superhero with an arsenal of superpowers at my disposal. *Unlike* many children, I used to love going to bed at night because of my superpower dreams; I could fly, jump high and long, swim like a dolphin, walk through walls, and more. Between my dreams and daydreams, I spent my youthful years saving the world. As a grown-up, when I try to lift a heavy object or assemble a complicated piece of gear, I have fond memories of my phantom superpowers of yesteryear.

As a teen, I kept that hero theme, inspired by the achievements of world-class athletes, inventors, leaders, and creative people such as Walt Disney. I wanted to know how they did what they did, where they found their ability to achieve such amazing feats. I felt they must have had some superpowers that helped them achieve such greatness.

My lifelong fascination with achievers inspired me to study personal development and human dynamics—including the understanding and application of personal power.

Personal Power: the "Achievement Ingredient"

Look up the word *power* in a dictionary, and you'll find a description such as "the ability or capacity to act, do, or influence in order to accomplish something." The idea is very simple, and we all can "act, do, or influence." Whether we do it is another story. I firmly believe that *personal power* is our willingness to act, exert our will, and apply our abilities so we can influence or achieve significant outcomes in our lives. Your personal power (or more specifically, your willingness to exercise or harness those abilities you have) plays a major role in what you achieve, especially in challenging times or crises.

Personal power isn't a mysterious force only known or owned by a few. We apply our personal power daily in many ways, moment to moment—practicing restraint in difficult conversations, exercising leadership, teaching our children by example and not just words, or encouraging ourselves to take a risk or make a difficult decision. These are all examples of acting, doing, and influencing your world. From the simple to the complicated, whenever you act or have some effect on a person or situation, you are exercising your personal power. Whenever you take the easy way out, instead of stepping up to the plate and taking charge in a situation requiring action, you relinquish your personal power.

Here's the good news for all of us "average" people—those who exercise their personal power as a matter of course are not superheroes nor are they endowed with any superpowers. They might seem self-confident, independent, and resourceful to admiring bystanders, but don't think they were born that way. For these people, being "comfortable in their skin" comes from taking risks, trying new experiences, and learning from both their successes and mistakes.

We all have a storehouse of innate skills, talents, and abilities in varying degrees, and each of these abilities can be enhanced, improved, and perfected. Please take me literally when I state that, eventually, with practice (trial and error), harnessing and applying your personal power will come naturally and require little effort once you hone your skills.

The issue with personal power is that too many people fail to recognize its existence, importance, or potential. As a life coach, repeatedly, I see in my clients a rich, untapped resource lying inert and unidentified. Their personal power, a payload of possibility, is always there, waiting to be acknowledged and applied.

The Powers that Be

I consider personal power an internal supply of God-given abilities and innate skills we consciously or unconsciously use on a daily basis—and often times don't realize their potential. Consider, for example, the power of attitude and thought. Our self-perception affects how we view the world and others, positively or negatively. For example, if we don't know how to access our personal power, we might feel helpless in a crisis, but the ability to stay calm in an emergency can help us avoid added trouble or tragedy. Think about how the power of resilience lets us heal or rebound after a setback. Consider the power of love and the miracles that occur because of faith, belief, and unconditional commitment. Reflect on how the power of empathy, connection, and compassion can ease an aching heart and radiate light on the darkness of despair or grief. Then, there's the power of choice, which I consider the super fuel of action and influence, the most potent personal power.

I recently witnessed a profound example of personal power applied in all these capacities when my brother Edgar lost his son, Alex. Only 20, Alex suddenly and unexpectedly died in his sleep. As you can imagine, it was a great shock to our entire family but mostly to his parents. Although it is profoundly painful to lose a child, the hurt intensifies when one dies so young. One feeling our entire family shared was in knowing that Alex was a very special human being. He was a kind and loving young man who brought much joy into the lives of others, and knowing this about him brought both grief and comfort.

We have many Powers that Be.

In the days following Alex's death, as we went through the wake and funeral, I was present with our family and friends as we grieved. Knowing I was in the midst of writing this book, not only was I caught up in the moment, but I also allowed myself to take things in as an observer.

I witnessed many people giving of themselves as they offered heartfelt condolences to my brother and our family. Caring friends and extended family members each accessed different aspects of their personal power, expressing compassion and sympathy for the parents and grandparents who most needed it. Watching my brother Edgar through those trying days and proceedings was a deeply touching experience.

Despite his extreme pain and grief, Edgar dug deep into his reservoir of personal power so he could compassionately comfort his ex-wife, Alex's mother. I couldn't help thinking that a lesser man might have withdrawn, blamed, or avoided offering such sweet acts of mercy. Consider the elements of personal power Edgar exercised so he could rise to the occasion.

My brother's example offers a glimpse into the potential power we all have. You've had your moments, and I wish even more for you in the future. My hope is that you realize your inner store of personal power and that you are fully using and exercising your great God-given gifts to achieve what you want and deserve in life. The point is that I encourage you to tap consciously into your personal power daily to expand your capacity so when you hit a small or a significant transition in your life, self-confidence and clear choice will be there, ready to propel you forward.

Personal Power: Use, It, Don't Lose It

As I interact with people around the world I'm taken aback at how often people either deny or give up their personal power without questioning and challenging themselves or considering the consequences. As a confessed student of human nature, I see a disturbing amount of denial or a relinquishing of personal power in intimate relationships. I know that fear is at the root of inaction. Consequently, we become paralyzed rather than proactive.

I witness men who won't admit their unhappiness, as if they are so fearful of their wife or partner's anger. Instead of speaking out, they let things slide, becoming unhappier and more discontent until they can't stand it anymore. In time, the man might become verbally or even physically abusive; he might eventually leave without warning or have an affair.

Then, some women are dominated subtly or overtly by the men in their lives. I once knew a woman who was not "allowed" to make decisions on her own. Whether a situation affected her alone, the children, or the whole family, her husband's stamp of approval was always required. In both these examples, think about what is sacrificed for the sake of not making waves. Not only is there an immediate loss of personal power, self-esteem, and respect from the other party, this lack of autonomy reflects some serious dysfunction that can ruin the relationship in the end. The stakes are high when we give up our personal power.

We've all had moments when we didn't dare break out of the mold for fear of the outcome, which helps us have some empathy for people who feel trapped in an unworkable relationship (or job or other circumstances). Unfortunately, inaction translates into maintaining the status quo. Whether we're discussing relationships, careers, or health maintenance, no change means no chance of improvement. Depending on how extreme the consequences might be, that can ultimately equate with no hope. What a waste of potential this is because when we allow circumstances to be so limiting, the circle of possibility contracts instead of expands.

We often stop ourselves from doing what we want or need because we don't think we have the right to act, or we lack the confidence to take the risk. We might fear that we'll alienate someone, end up in an even more precarious position, or lose face. I encourage you to push yourself when you face challenging circumstances so you can learn what your potential is.

Language is often a giveaway for when we're backing away from our personal power. Listen for statements such as "I just can't see myself doing that," or "I don't dare say (do) that." If you hear yourself or someone else utter a helpless or hopeless phrase, let it be a signal to stop and rethink the situation so you can move forward, not backward.

When I hear someone make seemingly innocent statements such as, "Oh, well, that's just the way it goes...," "Hey, what else could I have done..." or "Given the circumstances, I had no choice but to cave...," I wince. I see the shaking head and shrugging shoulders as signs of someone who gave away his or her personal power. It truly is a question of use it or lose it. In other words, when in doubt, move toward your personal power, not away from it.

Name It and Claim It

So dare I ask, how about you? In the "crunch" times, are you more likely to give in or get on with it? When you find yourself in a challenging situation or transition, do you reach inside, collect yourself, and rally your personal power, or do you back off and tell yourself it's just not worth the effort? I encourage you to consider the enormous stockpile of near-superpower and potential you have within your body, mind, and soul.

If we could harness the mental, physical, and spiritual energy housed in our beings, we could probably light a city the size of Milwaukee! OK, I might be stretching things a bit, but it's not a stretch to say that you have great untapped power and ability just waiting to be channeled toward your goal. Think of a horse and rider approaching the highest fence in a jumping competition. It might look impossibly high, but by harnessing their combined power, experience, and confidence, the pair clears the obstacle. You can do the same.

When I bring up the subject of personal power in my presentations, people aren't always clear on exactly what personal power is or what it represents. If I ask for a definition of "personal power," I get many stares and silence. If I ask my participants to consider how much personal power they have, most of them seem stumped. And when I ask for a recent example of when someone applied his or her personal power to meet a challenge, people look at me as if my hair is on fire.

Sometimes, a facet of life is so obvious that we don't even think about it or have a name for it. My point is that when you don't recognize, or fail to harness your potential fully, you limit your capacity for starting or navigating change. Well, you have a phenomenal storehouse of personal power, and if you're not using it, get on board and buckle your seatbelt. You're in for a whole new ride!

Harness Your Personal Power

My friend Bodo Gross is my favorite musician and songwriter. In his songs, Bodo uses colloquialisms and metaphors suggesting a depth of meaning beyond the obvious. His analogies are easy to identify with, which I find a bit amusing as my friend was born, raised, and still lives in his home country of Germany. English might be his second language, but you'd never know it listening to his music.

In his song "Message Part One," Bodo uses the phrase "Harness your horse... your choices are few." When I asked Bodo what this phrase meant to him, he explained that in attempting to move our life forward, we don't always have many choices. But my friend is convinced that two choices always exist. We can choose to harness the horse, which means we'll have control over the direction it takes... or not. If we don't put on the harness, we lose control, and the horse can go wherever it wants. This song makes me think of the out-of-control moments we suffer when our imaginative minds run amok. It takes experience, self-awareness, and self-confidence to let our personal power take charge in such circumstances.

Risk, Reward, or Recovery

I will be the first to admit that it's difficult even *thinking* about taking a risk when you already feel vulnerable and besieged by circumstances. But to be realistic, we take risks every day of our lives. Opening a can of food, driving on a highway, or taking a prescribed medicine are some everyday ways we put ourselves at risk.

When you are in emotional turmoil, you'll need to take some risks so you can bring your life back into a semblance of order. You know in your heart of hearts that if you don't take charge of your circumstances, like Bodo's horse without a harness, the unresolved situation could spin out of control and run away with you. Your solution will hinge on your action, and your plan will hinge on the risks you are willing to take. And the risks you're willing to take hinge on how you perceive your storehouse of personal power.

Risk can result in rewards or consequences, and we must be willing to accept either outcome without feeling smug (in the case of reward) or self-critical (if things don't work out). As children, we were punished when we risked unacceptable behaviors. As adults, we might be censured at work for expressing an unpopular opinion. We risk creating conflict with our spouse by broaching a touchy topic. Or we might lose money by taking a financial risk that doesn't work.

Move toward your personal power, not away from it.

As children, we took risks without considering the consequences, but with age, most of us tend to become more circumspect. When you were young, maybe you loved climbing trees, and you happened to live near an apple orchard, as I did. What a powerful feeling it was to scramble toward the top where you could snatch one of the ripest apples! Granted, risk was involved, but you were small and light, and the branches could hold you. Imagine the consequences if you tried to climb that tree today now that you've grown to full adult scale.

You might stand there and contemplate about how long it's been since you climbed a tree, wondering how far you could climb before you reached a branch that would break under your weight. You know more now; you've experienced both the rewards and consequences of risk taking. But knowing what you do doesn't mean you no longer take chances. It means you're smarter now, and you have a broader perspective; you know enough to trade childish impulsiveness for adult intentionality. You know how to plan, calculate, and execute your plan. You have the ability and will to propel yourself toward, through, and beyond life's challenges.

When you find yourself facing a transition, you might feel as if you've already stretched your comfort zone to the max, and the thought of pushing yourself further might be too much. On the other hand, you know that people who fear the unknown, those who fear change, tend to be stuck in the Gap, which is not a choice you want. Similar to my boyhood moment of hanging on to that huge pipe spanning the gorge, you might find yourself where you aren't sure about going forward, but going back isn't a suitable choice, either. To traverse that gaping void, that vast unknown area, you'll have to trust yourself and take some risks. Just as adversity so often brings learning and growth, taking a risk can yield rewards.

I'm not suggesting that you take foolish chances. I encourage you to look for the favorable or desirable circumstances you can create. You might have to get outside your comfort zone, climb that trunk, and reach that proverbial limb to find and grasp the opportunities awaiting you.

So how do you find the opportunities—the juiciest fruit? I say, look up! During times of difficulty, we tend to travel with our heads down, literally and figuratively. Sometimes, we become so preoccupied and self-absorbed with our situation that we fail to look around for all the possibilities that exist. I encourage you to maintain as broad a perspective as possible so you don't limit your choices or your inner ability to take positive action.

It's All in Your Mind

Many years ago, while I was living in California, a member of my church was arrested for public drunkenness. Understandably, he was very embarrassed when the news became public, and thinking that people would judge, reject him, or talk behind his back, he quit attending services. Although no one, as a practicing Christian, condoned his behavior, no one condemned him, either. But none of us had a chance to show our support because the man chose to avoid us. In effect, he relinquished his personal power by staying away.

The longer he stayed away the more convinced he became that we would ostracize or shun him. This man's perceptions were built on flawed assumptions that he never tested nor questioned; in his heart, he felt it was impossible to rebuild his reputation. This gives you a sense of how easy it can be to give up on ourselves instead of standing up to a difficult situation.

Finally, a few members of our church took the initiative and visited the man, letting him know they still cared about him and were concerned about his wellbeing. Their compassion helped him realize that he had chosen a lonesome, self-reinforcing path to powerlessness. Think of the long-term unhappiness this man could have suffered from his unwillingness to take charge of his circumstances. Instead of reaching out and/or facing his church friends, this member drove himself into unnecessary isolation where he felt helpless and hopeless. Without this caring intervention, the man would have continued to live in a lonely, closed loop of his own making.

Major transitions or other challenging events can put your perceptions to task. Exercising your personal power requires that you explore, challenge, and clarify your perceptions and feelings so you can avoid the unnecessary heartache of errors in judgment. It takes courage to face the aspects of reality that might pinch a bit. Better to experience self-imposed short-term discomfort instead of needlessly condemning yourself to long-term pain from which you might never recover.

When you have some "fence to mend," I encourage you to stop periodically and ask yourself, "Are my perceptions of this situation (or person) real, or is my interpretation based on ego or fear?" Summon your personal power by asking challenging questions such as "How do I know my perceptions are accurate—am I taking in the whole picture?" Probe as deeply as you can and ask, "Where or when have I had similar perceptions and feelings, and what were the results?"

Ask for the opinions and perspectives of trusted friends or family. This empowering approach helps you not only know yourself better, but also to be honest about what's going on in your head. Don't give your power away; don't be like the man who erected obstacles by thinking that self-isolation was his only choice. It's tempting to feel as if you're in a box canyon when your world starts closing in, but back up and study the situation from all sides. By maintaining an open and objective frame of mind, you'll be able to discover more choices and possibilities than you thought existed.

Let the Force Be with You

Never underestimate the magnificent power of your "heart" and mind. Acknowledging and exercising your personal power maximizes your ability to access the best of your mental faculties. Without false bravado or ego, you acknowledge and accept that you can overcome difficult times, that you can successfully take on and take charge of the challenges you might face.

Last fall, my youngest daughter Alexandra experienced the power of her mind and learned about "digging deep" into her reservoir of personal power. She was very nervous about playing in a tennis tournament against a player who was known to be one of the area's best players in her age category. Further, she had lost pretty badly to this player the last couple of times they played. However, before the match, my wife, her older sister (a strong player), and I encouraged her to work on being calm and relaxed, to stay focused on her game, not to worry about who was on the other side, and to stay positive—these being aspects of personal power.

Although the match did not start so well for her, we could literally see Alexandra trying to do the things we all talked about. Then, somewhere about the middle of the match, Alexandra started hitting the ball differently. She was hitting harder and with much greater precision than we had ever witnessed. The next thing we knew—while she was already a good player—she was playing at a much higher level and one we hardly recognized.

Harness your horse … your choices are few. (Bodo Gross)

Although, in the end, she lost the match to a very good player, she learned a lifelong lesson. She learned about personal power. She discovered that, in addition to hard work and good instruction, she had a source of energy and power she could "call on." It's like "the force" (if you will) from the movie *Star Wars.* You can't see it, and it's hard to explain, but once you tap into it, it takes you to a higher level of performance.

Your personal power is a powerhouse of unlimited potential you can draw from whenever the need arises. You already know this; you've done it in the past. You also know that the more you summon and exercise your inner power, the more trust and confidence you will have in yourself. You want to choose this self-perpetuating cycle in times of strife because this one will continue to expand your world instead of limiting it. It's all about growth, and growth is power.

Summary of "Harnessing Your Personal Power":

- *Personal power* is our willingness to act, exert our will, and apply our abilities so we can influence or achieve significant outcomes in our lives.
- Whenever you take the easy way out, instead of stepping up to the plate and taking charge in a situation requiring action, you relinquish your personal power.
- We all have an abundance of skills, talents, and abilities—each can be enhanced, improved, and perfected.
- We have many *Powers that Be.*
- The power of resilience lets us heal or rebound after a setback.
- People too often deny or give up their personal power.
- Inaction translates into the status quo.
- No change means no chance of improvement.
- Move toward your personal power, not away from it.
- When you fail to harness your potential fully, you limit your capacity for navigating change.
- Harness your horse... your choices are few. (Bodo Gross)
- Your solution will hinge on your action, and your plan will hinge on the risks you are willing to take.
- How do you find the "juiciest fruit?" Look up.
- Dress up, show up, and leave the rest to God.
- Trust the power of prayer.

Personal Reflections:

1. List your skills, talents, and abilities.

   - Are you using them to their fullest?
   - What can you do to enhance or improve them?
   - How can you draw on them to help you through your current or anticipated transition?

2. Inaction leads to the status quo.

   - Do you tend to act or accept the status quo?
   - Why do you accept the status quo? Fear of change? Fear of risk? It's comfortable?
   - Would you like to change?
   - What would it take to make you accept more risk?

3. Do you tend to take charge, or do you often relinquish your personal power because it's easier?

4. What steps are you willing to take to assert your personal power better?

Chapter 10

A Way Forward

"When I was going through my transition of being famous, I tried to ask God, why was I here? What was my purpose? Surely, it wasn't just to win three gold medals. There has to be more to this life than that."

— Wilma Rudolph

Finding Purpose

Major transitions *will* occur in our lives, whether we want them or not. Some of these changes we will choose; others (it seems) will choose us. From small adjustments to major shifts, we need to be open, adaptable, and as grounded as possible. Some changes or challenges you decide to take on might directly connect to your life's purpose. On the other hand, some changes imposed on you by circumstance or fate might end up making your purpose on this Earth far clearer, more vivid, or change your path altogether. The intensity of your transition can radically shift your perspective and turn you in a direction you never would have dreamed.

As I mentioned early in the book, change is inevitable; growth is optional. This is a truth I urge you to understand and act on. Whether you're in a Gap or anticipating a transition, *choose* to learn, grow, and find more meaning in life.

Finding Purpose in Traumatic Change and Transition

John Walsh, the host of *America's Most Wanted* found his life's purpose because of a major life transition. After the tragic abduction and brutal murder of his six-year-old son, John and his family began a campaign to help missing and exploited children. Their efforts eventually led to new legislation—the Missing Children Act of 1982 and the Missing Children's Assistance Act of 1984. Thanks to his activism and TV show, John Walsh has been instrumental in apprehending criminals whom might otherwise have never been caught. It's highly unlikely that John Walsh would have ever found this calling in life had he not experienced the tragic loss of his son.

Other people have ended up taking similar paths. Nancy Grace found her purpose of pursuing justice for victims of crime after the mugging and murder of her fiancé. Marc Klaas, father of the kidnapped and murdered Polly Klaas in Northern California, a frequent guest on Grace's program, follows his purpose with passion—that of making the world a safer place for kids.

The catastrophic events in each of these individuals' lives created a massive transition in which they found their life's work, their mission, the life-changing cause they will pursue for the rest of their lives. These are only three examples. Millions of people are, in their own way, doing great things because of a monumental event that changed them forever.

The event (change) is what *triggers* the shift. The subsequent soul-searching and attempts to put meaning back into life open up a new direction that likely would not have happened otherwise. This growth and learning I keep describing takes place when we traverse the Gap with heightened awareness, intentionality, and purpose.

Although it is odd that tragedy seems to teach more transformational lessons than triumph does, I'm not at all suggesting that you must encounter tragedy to find your life's work. It's not so much the tragedy in and of itself, but rather the impact and profoundness of the "jolt." Life-altering events can shake you to your core and unhinge all your preconceived notions. This "shaking up" causes you to stop, step back, question things much deeper, and to "see" differently. Thus, the

> *Difficult life change and transition may end up making your purpose on this earth far more clear.*

process of emerging through a difficult transition by way of introspection, contemplation, reflection, heightened self-awareness, the looking forward, the looking backward and in the moment, and seeing things with a different set of eyes—all these things coming together at once causes a "shift" that wouldn't happen in our normal life. The shift is the beginning of the journey toward greater enlightenment—that is, you gain clarity about life, your life, and your purpose, if you're searching.

So, if you have experienced, or you are in the midst of a traumatic change/transition, what will you do? Some are not tuned in enough (that is, self-aware) and therefore won't get the shift. Others keep looking back only to gain more bitterness about the loss, and others just give up or give in to the grief, perhaps never to truly complete their transition.

I want you to believe in the human spirit. I want you do dig deep, at the right time. However, I can't say enough that I don't minimize or lack the appreciation that where there is trauma and grief, it might take time for the wounds to heal enough to feel like moving on. Yet, at some point in your transition, I want you to see or create the shift. Search and focus on a positive outcome, the profound learning that comes from deep and challenging experiences.

I want you to find meaning where there seems to be none.

What About the Not So Traumatic Transitions?

I must admit that, in some ways, it's easier to discuss the difficult transitions. And truth be told, in my work and writings, I tend to gravitate or lean toward helping those having the most difficult transitions. However, I often remind myself—and now want to remind or acknowledge to you—that all transitions aren't dark and filled with grief.

Further, many transitions come from a more or less positive change in life, but can still be challenging and difficult; for instance a desired job change, graduating high school or college, marriage, and so forth. Some transitions begin as "negative" but turn out to be unimaginably positive. Others begin as a positive change but become amazingly difficult—for all the reasons mentioned earlier in the book. This was the case with my transition from the military, the one that spawned this book.

There are some things to consider when it comes to the less than traumatic transitions or even the altogether "positive" transitions. One, *all* transitions—good, bad, neutral, short, or long—offer opportunity for self-discovery and personal growth. As I suggested, epiphanies and shifts don't only come after "hitting rock bottom." You just have to look harder.

All transitions offer the opportunity to shift—to gain a new or unique perspective—and getting a different perspective has great value. A few years ago, my older daughter (Christina) and I went on a church mission trip to Nicaragua. This ten-day trip brought to both of us a perspective that forever changed our lives. We both realized a few things. First, how different real poverty looked. I've witnessed poverty, but not like in Nicaragua. Seeing these people suffer and without some of the basic things that we in the U.S. take for granted gave both of us a different attitude—we became grateful

> *The shift is the beginning of the journey toward greater enlightenment.*

for our lives. Second, however, we noticed how happy most people seemed. In some ways, it was hard to understand—happiness under such impoverished conditions? But, of course, this notion helped us with our perspective—that "stuff" doesn't equal happiness. No doubt, they want and need more to make their lives *better*, but not *happier*. My daughter and I experienced a brief and limited glimpse into another [new] world. This experience shifted our perspective on life in a positive and lasting way, making us better people.

As an aside, I also had a shift as to how I saw my daughter Christina—and frankly "teenagers" as a whole. We ("I") sometimes think that teenagers are shallow and think only about material possessions. However, throughout the course of this mission trip through her actions and comments she (and other teens) showed a maturity and depth that I hadn't noticed before. It revealed the incredible person she is and the great potential she has as a human being. I'll forever see her (and teenagers) differently—from an *even more* positive viewpoint.

A Way Forward

At first, I titled this chapter (and paragraph), "The Way Forward," but in thinking about it, I had to acknowledge that in life (and therefore transitions), there is no single way forward. For many things in life, there aren't definitive maps. Life—and therefore transitions—is a journey; and although many can and

Find meaning where there appears to be none.

will help along the way, much of your journey you must figure out by and for yourself. The *journey* and the struggle—and the "how" you walk it— make the biggest difference.

Over the years, I've paid attention and asked many questions about life and what it takes to be successful—and you've likely guessed what I've discovered. That's right; many keys unlock the variety of doors to success. And these keys (or fundamental premises) are the same for being successful through any life transition. All you've read offers much of what I've learned, but here are a few parting thoughts.

Parting Thoughts

In reading this book, I hope you have a better sense of some important aspects of personal change and transition. Here are a few parting thoughts:

1. *The Gap* is that tenuous transitional phase between the old world and new. Transitions are part of life. There are practical and psychological aspects to transition. The psychological part is often the most difficult.

2. *Many types and sizes of Gaps* (transitions) and many factors influence the intensity of a transition. However, all transitions offer opportunities for personal growth and self-discovery to occur, if you are open to change.

3. *Change is an event; the transition is a journey and process.* As much as you can, it is important that you allow the transition to occur. When things get uncomfortable, don't panic; look the fear in the eyes and try to deal with it. Slay those drag-ons, those things (emotions) that drag you down and/or hold you back.

4. *Don't rush through or become irrational during a major transition.* Take the time to slow down, stop, step back, and gain perspective about your life and your direction in life.

5. *Your mind can be your best friend but also your worst enemy.* Before or during a major transition, try to develop your mental toughness. You can do so by attending to your perceptions, managing your expectations, and choosing your attitude. Although you must pay attention to the problems you encounter, focus on solutions. This will keep you from being stuck.

6. *Pay attention to how you think and talk* (to yourself). Recognize that we all have self-limiting thoughts and beliefs, but also know that you can overcome them by replacing negative statements with confidence-building affirmations, by surrounding yourself with positive and proactive people, through positive prayers and meditation, and by taking action. This will help you harness your personal power and use the Gap to find, redefine, or refine your purpose and make the most of life's "opportunities."

7. *When dealing with grief, don't rush the process.* However, when it's time, move on. In the meantime, allow people to love and take care of you. If you've gained wisdom and insight about dealing with adversity... pass it on.

A Few More Thoughts

Your thoughts and beliefs matter... as they shape your motives for and actions in life. They shape who you are and why you do the things you do. If there is a "key"—this is it. Be careful about what you think and believe. Work toward clearing your mind of all your baggage. I can tell you from experience, this is likely a lifelong struggle, but every "bag" you shed allows for a lighter load and more energy to put toward better use.

Your vision matters... because the clearer you are about where you are going in life, the better the chances you'll have of getting to your final destination. Again, this premise applies to major life transitions. When the time is right, try to envision your end in mind. See it, crystallize it, and then go after it.

Your desire matters... You've heard it a million times how someone achieved great success through perseverance. Perseverance, tenacity, self-motivation, discipline, and these sorts of personal attributes are necessary, but they don't seem to be inherent in us all. So, if you weren't lucky enough to be born with them... then what? Unfortunately, there's not a great answer. It means you have to try harder, find a way, and/or get a coach—someone to push you. Ultimately, you must keep trying to go beyond what you "feel" like doing. It might take a little longer, but even small steps and fragmented efforts amount to something greater.

Keep going... You can do it!

About the Author

For more than twenty years, Kevin Richard McNulty has worked as a personal development coach and speaker, helping thousands of people discover (or revisit) simple but powerful truths about learning, changing, growing, and achieving lifelong goals. From established executives to those still searching for their place in life, Kevin's skillful coaching and high impact presentations offer effective strategies for continuing personal or professional development.

Through his speaking and writing, Kevin moves people to a higher level of understanding and comfort with some more difficult or challenging aspects of work and life. His expertise includes managing change and navigating through significant transitions as well as other topics related to human and organizational dynamics.

While his formal education includes a Master's in Communications/Leadership and Influence, Kevin believes that his real education and hard-won wisdom come from experiences and observations drawn from an extraordinary life. His diverse life experience includes an immersion into an international lifestyle—being raised in Bavaria, Puerto Rico, and various regions around the U.S.—as well as a unique career within the U.S. Air Force and extensive travels around the U.S.,

Europe, Pacific Region, and the Middle East. In his lifetime, Kevin has relocated more than twenty times. Professionally, he has traveled to forty-nine states and twenty-five countries, served in a diplomatic capacity at the U.S. Embassy in Tel Aviv, Israel, and even performed in a Super Bowl Halftime Show. These and many more unusual experiences have contributed to his broad knowledge base and unique understanding of life, culture, and human dynamics.

Currently, Kevin is the founder and CEO of Humadyn-Life Skills Institute. He coaches and speaks around the world on many topics, including change, personal/professional development, and a range of business-related topics such as leadership, workplace dynamics, cultural relations, communications, and conflict resolution. His mission is to help people think deeper, see more clearly, and make informed decisions, so they can take meaningful steps toward accomplishing their goals and achieving their dreams.

Kevin lives with his wife Jane and two daughters (Christina and Alexandra) near Nashville, Tennessee.

You can learn with and/or contact Kevin at
www.thegapbetweentwoworlds.com
www.humadyn.com/ and
www.facebook.com/thegapbetweentwoworlds

Kevin@humadyn.com
615-216-0481 ext. 33

We hope you have been inspired, empowered
and encouraged by your journey through
The Gap Between Two Worlds.

If so, please refer us to your family and friends.

👍Like us on Facebook.com/TheGapBetweenTwoWorlds

To order additional copies:

- Visit our website www.thegapbetweentwoworlds.com

- Call *615-216-0481 ext. 55*

- Complete and mail the form below

   *We accept cash, credit cards, personal checks
   (made out to Kevin McNulty) and money orders.*

--cut along line----

The Gap Between Two Worlds Mail Order Form

Please send me ____ *(Quantity)* Softcover books at $16.95 each *(tax included)* = _____

Please send me ____ *(Quantity)* Hardcover books at $19.95 each *(tax included)* = _____

Discount available for large orders. Call 615-216-0481 ext. 55

+ Shipping & Handling $5

TOTAL Enclosed $_____

Shipping Address: Name: _____

Street:_____ City: _____

State: _____ Zip: _____ Phone *(including area code):* _____

Email Address: _____

If paying by credit card: (Visa and MasterCard accepted)

Card Number: _____ Expiration: _____

Security Code (from back): _____ Name on Card: _____

Billing Address *(if different than shipping address)*

Street: _____ City: _____

State: _____ Zip: _____

Mail form, along with your enclosed payment, to:

Humadyn-Life Skills Institute, P.O. Box 331521, Murfreesboro, TN 37133

THANK YOU!

Scan to "Like" us on Facebook.

CPSIA information can be obtained at www.ICGtesting.com
Printed in the USA
LVOW12s0131240216

476466LV00003B/5/P